1,00,-

Population Economics

Titels in the Series

Jacques J. Siegers · Jenny de Jong-Gierveld
Evert van Imhoff (Eds.)
Female Labour Market Behaviour and Fertility

Hendrik P. van Dalen
Economic Policy in a Demographically Divided World

Dieter Bös · Sijbren Cnossen (Eds.)
Fiscal Implications of an Aging Population

Klaus F. Zimmermann (Ed.)

Migration and Economic Development

With 10 Figures

Springer-Verlag
Berlin Heidelberg New York London Paris Tokyo
Hong Kong Barcelona Budapest

Professor Dr. Klaus F. Zimmermann
Universität München
Seminar für Arbeits- und Bevölkerungsökonomie
Ludwigstr. 28 RG
W-8000 München 22, FRG

ISBN 3-540-55557-9 Springer-Verlag Berlin Heidelberg New York Tokyo
ISBN 0-387-55557-9 Springer-Verlag New York Berlin Heidelberg Tokyo

2142/7130-543210 - Printed on acid-free paper

Preface

Klaus F. Zimmermann

Migration has become a topic of substantial interest in Europe in recent years. Part of this interest is driven by the important political changes in East Europe and the potential threat of large East-West migration waves. However, due to the large differences in economic development a substantial migration pressure is also expected from the South of Europe as of other parts of the world. The global migration potential towards the higher developed areas has reached about 80 to 100 million people. Thereof, about 60 million would like to move permanently, 20 million temporarily and about 15 million are refugees and asylum seekers and approximately 30 million are illegals.

The book consists of eight papers which are allocated to five parts: Theoretical Models (Part I), Performance of Migrants (Part II), Migration Within Developing Countries (Part IV) and Immigration Policy (Part V). Each paper begins with a brief summary of its content. Part I, *Theoretical Models*, contains first "A Microeconomic

Model of Migration" by Siegfried Berninghaus and Hans-Günther Seifert-Vogt. They study migration decision making under incomplete information and apply it to empirically relevant phenomena. The second paper by Gerhard Schmitt-Rink "Migration and International Factor Price Equalization" demonstrates that international migration tends to equalize national factor prices and factor shares even in the absence of international trade.

In Part II, *Performance of Migrants*, Lucie Merkle and Klaus F. Zimmermann study "Savings and Remittances: Guestworkers in West Germany". They show that savings and remittances of guestworkers are negatively related to the planned duration of residence in the host country, but only the relationship with remittances is statistically significant. In Part III, *Effects of Emigration on the Sending Country*, Thomas Straubhaar presents evidence on the "Impact of International Labor Migration for Turkey". He concludes that emigration only under certain preconditions may influence positively the economy of the sending country.

Part IV, *Migration Within Developing Countries*, contains first a contribution on "Rural-Urban Migration. On the Allocation of Risks in Developing Countries" by Renate Schubert. She demonstrates that the allocation of individual and collective risks is sub-optimal in rural-urban migration in developing countries. The second paper is "Place of Birth and Past Place of Residence in South Korea: Methodological Considerations for Migration Research" by Joachim Singelmann and Jiang Hong Li. It evaluates the possibility of estimating immigration and net migration from information about place of birth by applying the census-survival-ratio method to life-time migration and finds no large improvement in comparison to applying the method to the general population.

Part V, *Immigration Policy*, contains two contributions: Christoph M. Schmidt and Klaus F. Zimmermann study "Migration Pressure in Germany: Past and Future". They find that West Germany had been an immigration country ever since the beginning of the fifties and a realistic evaluation of the potential East-West migration should conclude that the impact on Germany will not be critical. Jozef M. M. Ritzen and Hendrik P. van Dalen contribute a paper on "The Economic Consequences of Selective Immigration Policies". They study a selective immigration policy for both the country of immigration and emigration within a two-country economic growth model and show that an investment policy in human and physical capital is preferable in comparison to immigration.

The edition of a volume demands substantial efforts. I appreciated the dedicated help by Thomas Bauer, John De New, Lucie Merkle, Martin Mühleisen and Doris Müller. I also thank all contributors for their patience and constructive cooperation and the Springer-Verlag for making the publication possible.

Contents

I. Theoretical Models

A Microeconomic Model of Migration

Siegfried Berninghaus

Hans-Günther Seifert-Vogt

Abstract: In the first part of the paper we give a consistent formal model of migration decision making under incomplete information. It is shown that the migration problem can be regarded as a particular problem in the theory of stochastic dynamic programming. We discuss the Gittins index method as a helpful algorithm in deriving optimal migration decisions. In the second part of the paper we apply our theoretical results to two empirically relevant phenomena. We explain the "attractiveness of city lights" in rural/urban migration as a result of optimal decision making under incomplete information by using arguments that are different from Todaro's explanation. Further, we give an explanation for the high correlation between inbound and outbound migration that is often observed in particular regions in developing countries.

1. Introduction

During the past twenty years many economists became attracted by the theory of migration. It is the microeconomic aspect of migration theory that has been elaborated during these years. In the present paper we want to contribute to this aspect by introducing a microeconomic model of migration decision making under incomplete information. Our model turns out to be useful in explaining satisfactorily some important observable phenomena in migration (for details see Berninghaus and Seifert-Vogt (1987)). In applying our theoretical results, we put emphasis in the present paper on migration problems in less developed countries.

As a milestone in microeconomic theory, one can regard the well-known "Human-Capital" (H.C.) model of migration that was introduced by Sjaastad (1962) and has been developed further by many authors (e.g. Cebula (1979), Langley (1974), Hart (1975)). The basic idea of the H.C. approach is to regard migration as an investment that entails (migration) costs *now* in the hope of benefits in the *future*. In its simplest version a potential migrant has to calculate the discounted future income stream minus costs (over a given planning horizon) for each region and then moves to the region with the largest discounted net benefits. To make the model more realistic, one can assume that income includes not only monetary benefits but also non-wage income (as welfare payments, amenities etc.). Costs can be interpreted not only as transportation costs but also as opportunity costs of adapting to a new environment or as "psychological costs" of leaving friends and relatives etc. Compared with the existing economic theories of migration at that time, the H.C. approach proved to be superior by taking account of future and not only of monetary wage differentials. Even though the H.C. approach proved to be very popular for econometricians, it has a serious shortcoming, as uncertainty of the decision maker about future income and cost data is neglected.

This point has been emphasized for example by Todaro (1969) (respetively Harris and Todaro (1970)) in his path-breaking article on rural/urban migration in less developed countries. He modified the simple version of the H.C. model by considering expected discounted future income streams where the expected values in each period are represented as per-period wages multiplied by the probability to the unemployed. By this procedure, Todaro was able to explain the migration of farmers into the urban area although they might be unemployed there for a considerable period. If the expected wages were large enough, it would pay for a farmer to leave his home region according to the discounted expected value criterion, inspite of possible unemployment.

The problem with incorporating this kind of incomplete information into the H.C. model is obvious. It is not possible to formalize rational learning within this framework. Naturally, a decision maker facing incomplete information will gather information by migration itself and eventually will decide to return if he has a bad experience, for instance if he gets no job at all. Further if he is a rational decision maker, he will take account of possible remigration *before* migrating into another region. It is not possible to model this behaviour consistently within the traditional variants of the H.C. approach. Return migration and repeat migration, two relevant observable phenomena, should be explained as a result of rational decision making under incomplete information.

In recent years some authors concentrated on the incomplete imformation aspect of migration and tried to integrate the theory of job search with migration theory. Here, one can point out the important work of David (1974) or Maier (1985). Both authors assume that a potential migrant tries to reduce incomplete information by active job search in each region, which is not costless.

Although these models may be regarded as a substantial improvement of the traditional H.C. approach, they were not able to give a consistent explanation of remigration and other similar phenomena which should be considered as created by belated information. To overcome this shortcoming one should look for decision models incorporating potential later revisions of earlier decisions induced by incoming unfavourable information. A well-known paradigm in mathematical statistics — called "*Multi-armed Bandit*" — seems to be perfectly applicable to migration decision-making under incomplete information. According to this paradigm a decision maker has the opportunity to pursue at each decision time point one of a given finite number of "activities". Pursuing an activity for one period produces an (economic) reward, i.e. a random variable with unknown distribution. It is typical for Multi-armed Bandit problems that a decision maker gathers information about the reward probability law of each "arm" by pulling this arm. Consequently it may be wise for the decision maker to sacrifice some potential early pay-off for the prospect of gaining information that will allow for better informed choices later. In this respect a Multi-armed Bandit problem embodies a conflict inherent in all human action. It is the conflict between gathering information versus immediate pay-off.

Obviously a potential migrant is typically confronted with a situation described above. He is only incompletely informed about the returns to migration and typically can learn the characteristics of a region only by moving into the region at least for some time. After information has been gathered, he decides to change regions or to stay for another period according to his information. McCall and McCall (1984, 1987) were the first who applied Multi-armed Bandit solution techniques to the problem of migration decision making. Berninghaus and Seifert-Vogt (1987) extended McCall's model to a very general class of migration decision problems. In a recent paper Pessino (1987) applied a finite planning horizon version of the Two-armed Bandit with a two-period horizon to a migration decision problem. McCall's model and our model that will be presented below, utilize the so called "Gittins index Theory", which is a simplified solution method for a particular class of Multi-armed Bandit problems. It can be demonstrated that (see e.g. Gittins (1979), Wittle (1980), Berninghaus (1984)) the optimal policy in the Gittins index framework allows valuable insight into the economics of the underlying formal problem and furthermore has a simple structure. Depending on the state of information about each activity, there is a single real number (Gittins index) associated to each activity, such that the optimal policy is that activity with the largest index. It will be shown below that the Gittins index policy exhibits clear characterizations of the optimal migration policy; in particular it simplifies its comparative static analysis.

In the following chapter we will start with a stylized migration problem where a potential migrant is assumed to be incompletely informed about the pecuniary and non-pecuniary aspects of a given number of regions. He can improve his information about a region by active job search at the beginning of his stay in this region, but information about the non-pecuniary aspects typically will only come in later periods ("belated information"). After presenting the model we will give a brief outline of Gittins index theory, sufficiently general to solve the problem at hand, and we describe the optimal migration policy. In the last chapter we will apply our theoretical results to explain some selected problems concerning rural/urban migration in less developed countries.

2. A Microeconomic Model of Migration under Incomplete Information

In the following, we will present a model which is sophisticated enough to draw some interesting conclusions concerning migration behavior, while remaining simple enough to be analytically tractable[1]. It will be easily seen that some simplifications are made for expository purposes only, while other restrictions seem to be more serious. They will be discussed thoroughly in the following.

Now let us consider a potential migrant who has the choice of moving into one of N immigration regions[2] indexed by j. Four components are assumed to be relevant for the migration decision :

1) the wage w_j that can be earned in j

2) the moving costs k_j for moving into region j. They have to be interpreted here first of all as opportunity costs of searching when moving to an unknown place (generated by gathering information about shopping facilities, schooling, housing, etc.)

---

1 The formal structure of this model has been elaborated extensively in Berninghaus and Seifert-Vogt (1987).

2 The home region of the migrant is supposed to be one of the immigration regions.

3) the search costs c_j that are generated by job search activities in region j

4) the quality of life in region j that is — to simplify considerations — supposed here to be representable by a real number α_j. With respect to the quality of life, we summarize all factors that influence the subjective welfare of an individual after migration into the region; this may be the cultural climate in the region, the education system, the acceptance by the neighborhood, etc.

Furthermore, we assume that the migrant is completely informed about c_j and k_j (for each j) but is incompletely informed about w_j and α_j. To be more precise, the migrant is supposed to have a subjective probability distribution regarding w_j and α_j, with cumulative distribution functions denoted by $F_j(\cdot)$ and $G_j(\cdot)$. To improve his information, a migrant is allowed to search actively for a job in the first period of his stay in j. Then, he incurs search costs c_j, and at the end of the first period he knows w_j. From a formal point of view, the decision maker is allowed to draw a random sample in each region which is not costless from the population of jobs distributed according to $F_j(\cdot)$. Naturally, this is a rather crude picture of a job search process. One could incorporate more sophisticated job search models but this would only make insight into the structure of the optimal migration policy more difficult. To connect this assumption with the standard job search models, one could imagine for example that the distribution $F_j(\cdot)$ already results from performing a sophisticated job search strategy in region j.

Concerning the quality of life, we suppose that the migrant knows his realized α_j at the end of the second period of his stay in region j. This seems to be a realistic assumption as we interpret α_j as comprising of all the experiences that a migrant makes after living some time in region j, i.e., making friends, discovering the "cultural environment", etc. That is, we assume α_j is essentially delayed information. For the sake of simplicity, we suppose furthermore that α_j can be measured in monetary units such that the total return on migration into region j after two periods of living there is completely known and given by $(w_j + \alpha_j)$. Concentrating on a particular region j, we can illustrate the return and information process by the following diagram.

Obviously one could summarize the above procedure simply as follows: Before a potential migrant settles forever in an unknown region, he spends the first period searching for a job. After having found a job the migrant can decide to move into the region for at least one period, incurring moving costs k_j. At the end of the second period he is completely informed about all relevant aspects of the return in region j and he will earn $(w_j + \alpha_j)$ in each future period. It should be emphasized here that the migrant has the opportunity to leave region j after each period to "try out" another region. Naturally this would make sense only at the beginning of the information-gathering process in each region.

Concerning the distributions $F_j(\cdot)$ and $G_j(\cdot)$ we could assume either that job search and experience of quality of life constitute random experiments whose results are governed by $F_j(\cdot)$ and $G_j(\cdot)$ or that these distributions only display the heterogeneity between the migrants with respect to w_j and α_j. Further, the migrants do not

Figure 1:

Information and return structure of the migration process.

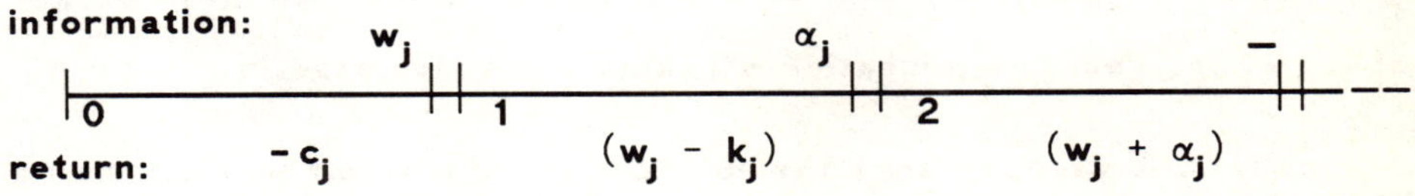

exactly know to which w_j and α_j class they belong. Regardless, the following derivations do not depend on the interpretations of $F_j(\cdot)$ and $G_j(\cdot)$. One only has to assume that from a formal point of view, some steps in the migration history of a migrant are connected with the realization of random variables W_j and A_j, whose distributions the migrants are supposed to know. Furthermore, these distributions might also differ from the *true* distributions denoted by $\overline{F}_j(\cdot)$ and $\overline{G}_j(\cdot)$, which will play a role only in the final chapter of our paper, where realized migration streams are calculated.

Finally, we suppose that the migrant is interested in maximizing the expected discounted returns on migration over his planning horizon. Therefore we are looking for a *migration policy* that is a prescription that tells the migrant which region to choose for living in each period such that the overall *expected discounted returns are maximized*. It should be emphasized here that in our concept of a migration policy, later revisions of a migration decision are naturally incorporated. Consequently, in determining an optimal policy one has to take later remigration decisions into account in the current time period. Finally, it should be remarked that the optimal migration policy depends on the state of information the migrant has about the regions in question at each decision time point. This will be demonstrated in the following chapter.

3. Optimal Migration Policies and Gittins Indices

In the present chapter we will reformulate the migration problem, presented above, as a Multi-armed Bandit (=MAB) problem. For this sake we need some further terminology that will be introduced immediately. First of all we have to define for each region a "state space" denoted by S_j, as the set of all possible information states about region j. Taking account of the fact that "no information" has also to be regarded as a state of information, we define for each region an artificial information state s_{oj} by

s_{oj} ..... "region j has not been visited before".

To motivate our particular definition of s_j, we remind one here of the information process caused by migration into region j, now supplemented by the information state s_{oj}, which can be illustrated by the following sketch.

$$s_{oj} \mapsto w_j \mapsto (w_j,\alpha_j) \longmapsto (w_j,\alpha_j) \vdash\!\!-\!\!-$$

If the decision maker decides to search for a job in region j, his state of information changes from s_{oj} to w_j ($\in \mathbb{R}$) which induces a change from w_j to $(w_j,\alpha_j) \in \mathbb{R}^2$, provided the decision maker decides to stay for a second period in region j. After this state of information has been reached, it does not change any more. Technically speaking, the decision maker has reached an "absorbing" state. According to the reasoning above it makes sense to define the state space[3] of region j as follows:

$$S_j := \{s_{oj}\} \cup \mathbb{R} \cup \mathbb{R}^2.$$

---

3 Technical remark: S_j should be regarded as a finite union of disjoint sets provided with its "final topology".

Now we can describe state transitions more precisely by a stochastic transition law, that is a transition probability on S_j, denoted by $P_j\ (\cdot|\cdot)$ and represented by its cumulative distribution function as follows:

$$P_j\ (w_j|s_{Oj}) := F_j(w_j)$$

$$P_j\big((w_j,\alpha_j)|w_j)\big) := G_j(\alpha_j)$$

$$P_j\big((w_j,\alpha_j)|(w_j,\alpha_j)\big) := 1.$$

Obviously, we need not consider other state transitions.

Up to now we have almost all ingredients to interpret the migration problem as a specialized Multi-armed Bandit problem. It remains to define a reward function $R_j(\cdot)$: $S_j \longrightarrow \mathbb{R}$ for each region, that associates to each state in S_j an (economic) reward. According to our model presented above, we define:

$$R_j\ (s_O) := -c_j,$$

$$R_j\ (w_j) := (w_j - k_j),$$

$$R_j\ \big((w_j,\alpha_j)\big) := (w_j + \alpha_j).$$

Now we are ready to interpret "migration into region j" as "pursuing activity j", characterized by S_j, $P_j(\cdot|\cdot)$ and $R_j(\cdot)$, in a Multi-armed Bandit problem[4]. In our special problem the decision maker is rather efficient in gathering information. After pulling an

4 Because of the definition of the transition probabilities given above we have a Multi-armed Bandit problem with "independent arms". The state transitions of one "arm" do not depend on the states of other "arms".

arm two times the decision maker is already supposed to be completly informed about the return of this arm.

To determine the optimal migration policy we will apply well-known results concerning optimal policies in Multi-armed Bandit problems (e.g. Berryand Fristedt (1985)). To simplify the optimal policy by using Gittins indices, we have to make the following crucial assumption concerning the development of states in S_k ($k \neq j$) when the decision maker is pursuing activity j.

(*) *If activity j is pursued for a given period, then the states of the remaining activities are frozen.*

Remark: The plausibility of this assumption depends on the interpretation of states in particular applications. In our migration model, where "state" of an activity is identified with a decision maker's "state of information", assumption (*) does not seem to be very restrictive, because a migrant living in region j, typically gets no reliable information about the quality of life and similar data in region k ($k \neq j$).

As Gittins was able to demonstrate, assumption (*) simplifies the structure of the optimal policy considerably. His result can be utilized for the derivation of the optimal migration policy as follows:

The basic idea of the so-called Gittins index policy is to reduce the solution complexity of the general migration problem to that of simpler (artificial) stopping problems. In doing this, one has to consider the following stopping problem for each region:

(SP) Suppose a state of information $s_j \in S_j$ given and the migrant has the option to live in j for a further period and then proceeding optimally or to retire from this decision problem with terminal payment Z_j.

If we denote by $V_j(Z_j;s_j)$ the maximal expected discounted return of the problem (SP) starting with s_j, then we have the following functional equation ($\beta \in (0,1)$ denotes the discount factor):

$$V_j(Z_j;s_j) = \max\left\{ Z_j; R_j(s_j) + \beta \int V_j(Z_j;s_j') \, dP_j(s_j'|s_j)\right\} \tag{1}$$

from which we can in principle derive the optimal stopping policy for the problem (SP) in each period. We are not interested in determining this policy, but we want to perform the following procedure: Determine Z_j such that the migrant is indifferent between staying for a further period and retiring from the decision problem. Let us denote this value by[5] $Z_j(s_j)$. Formally this value is determined by the following equation:

$$Z_j(s_j) = R_j(s_j) + \beta \int V(Z_j(s_j); s_j') \, dP_j(s_j'|s_j). \tag{2}$$

The real numbers $Z_j(s_j)$ will be called "Gittins indices"[6]. It can be demonstrated that, given the assumptions of our model, there always exists a unique solution of (2) (e.g. Berninghaus (1984)). Surprisingly, the Gittins indices turn out to be the central concepts in determining the optimal migration policy.

---

5 To emphasize its state-dependence.

6 Technical remark: It can be shown (see Mandelbaum (1986, p.145)) that $Z_j(\cdot): S_j \longrightarrow \mathbb{R}$ is measurable if S_j is provided with the appropriate topology. It can be demonstrated that the "final topology" on S_j, introduced before, will do.

Theorem (Gittins (1979, Whittle (1980/1982)):

Let there be given the migration problem described above and let assumption (*) be fulfilled. If at a given decision time point the state of information about each region is given by $\{s_j\}_1^N$*, then an optimal migration policy describes to live in region j* for the following period where j* is given by*

$$Z_{j*}(s_{j*}) = \max_j z_j(s_j).$$

Remarks: a) Although the Gittins-index policy considerably simplifies the calculation of the optimal policy, it may still be a difficult task to calculate $Z_j(s_j)$ in a given model.

b) It follows immediately from the above theorem that only the Gittins index of the region where the migrant is living may change while the Gittins indices of the other regions remain constant.

The proof of the theorem is not trivial. An illustrative proof of the validity of the Gittins index rule has been given in a special framework by Berninghaus and Seifert-Vogt (1987). It is not the purpose of this paper to analyze the proof of the important theorem, but nevertheless it might be useful to illustrate the intuitive plausibility of the Gittins index rule by a simple example below before we apply the theorem to migration theory in the following chapter.

Example

Let us consider a decision maker in a MAB framework who can choose pulling one of two arms at each decision time point. The first arm is deterministic in the sense that the decision maker obtains 5 monetary units per period if he pulls this arm, however he is incompletely informed about the return of the second arm. For the sake of simplicity, we assume that the decision maker knows that the return of the second arm is equal to 0 with *a priori* probability $\frac{1}{4}$ and equal to 10 with probability $\frac{3}{4}$. But he has to pay $-c$ ($c>0$) monetary units if he pulls the second arm for the first time. Furthermore, after pulling this arm for the first time, the decision maker is supposed to know the return (either 10 or 0) with certainty.

Now we are ready to calculate the optimal policy according to the theorem by looking at equation (1) and (2) above. To determine the Gittins index for the first arm we have to calculate $V_1(Z_1(\cdot),\cdot)$, which is obviously given by

$$V_1(Z_1(\cdot),\cdot) \equiv \max\left\{Z_1(\cdot), \frac{5}{1-\beta}\right\}.$$

Consequently, we have

$$Z_1(\cdot) \equiv \frac{5}{1-\beta}.$$

It is somewhat more difficult to calculate the Gittins index for the second arm as there is a state transition after the first pull of this arm. For ease of notation let us denote the value functions of pulling the second arm by

$$V_2(Z_2, s_o),\ V_2(Z_2, 0),\ V_2(Z_2, 10)$$

if arm 2 has not been pulled yet, if information on arm 2 has come in and implies that return on arm 2 is 0, and if information on arm 2 has come in and implies that return on arm 2 is 10.

According to (1) we have to solve the functional equation

$$V_2(Z_2,s_o) = \max\{Z_2(s_o),\ -c + \beta(\tfrac{1}{4}V_2(Z_2(s_o),\ 0) + \tfrac{3}{4}V_2(Z_2(s_o),\ 10))\} \quad (1')$$

By the same reasoning as above we obtain

$$V\big(Z_2(s_o),0\big) = Z_2(s_o)$$

$$V\big(Z_2(s_o),10\big) = \max\left\{Z_2(s_o),\ \frac{10}{1-\beta}\right\}$$

as the second arm gives a deterministic return from the second pull on. Consequently we determine $Z_2(s_o)$ from

$$Z_2(s_o) = -c + \beta\left(\tfrac{1}{4}Z_2(s_o) + \tfrac{3}{4}\max\left\{Z_2(s_o),\ \frac{10}{1-\beta}\right\}\right)$$

which results in[7]

$$Z_2(s_2) = \frac{-c}{\left(1-\frac{\beta}{4}\right)} + 7.5 \frac{\beta}{(1-\beta)\left(1-\frac{\beta}{4}\right)} \tag{2'}$$

Therefore it follows from the theorem that the decision maker will pull the unknown arm if $Z_2(s_2) > Z_1(s_0)$, that is after some manipulations, if the inequality

$$c < 7.5 \frac{\beta}{1-\beta} - 5 \frac{(1-\frac{\beta}{4})}{1-\beta} \tag{3}$$

is valid. Inequality (3) can be interpreted such that the decision maker obviously tries out the uncertain arm if the "experimenting costs" (here equal to c) are "sufficiently" low. This seems to be a plausible procedure if we furthermore take the fact that $Z_2(0) = 0$, $Z_2(10) = \frac{10}{1-\beta}$ into account, implying that the decision maker will change the arm if it turns out to be inferior after pulling it once.

For sake of completeness let us compare this optimal procedure with the traditional H.C. rule which requires arm 1 to be pulled at the beginning if[8]

$$\frac{7.5\beta}{1-\beta} - \frac{5}{1-\beta} < c. \tag{4}$$

---

7 The result is derived by setting primarily $Z_2(s_0) > \frac{10}{1-\beta}$ which implies $Z_2(s_0) = \frac{-c}{1-\beta}$, a contradiction. Consequently, we have to assume $Z_2(s_0) \leq \frac{10}{1-\beta}$ which gives the results above.

8 Here we use the H.C. rule with expected values for arm 2

Combining inequality (4) with (3) we can see that there always exists a whole interval of c such that (3) and (4) are fulfilled simultaneously, or in other words, that the H.C. rule proposes a suboptimal procedure. Intuitively this result illustrates drastically the weakness of the H.C. rule (even in its modified version with expected values) which excludes rational learning.

4. Migration in Less Developed Countries

Our model introduced above obviously is flexible enough to deal with different migration phenomena. As mentioned in the introduction, we will focus here on giving a decision theoretical foundation of some stylized facts on migration in less developed countries. More precisely we will concentrate here on two main topics concerning rural/urban migration:

- attractiveness of "city lights",
- strong correlation between in-migration and out-migration rates.

We will give explanations of these phenomena in the framework of our sequential migration model. However, before we can do this, we will give a preparatory discussion concerning further properties of the optimal migration policy. We will be especially interested in the comparative statics of the optimal migration policy.

4.1. Further characterization of the optimal migration policy

The structure of the optimal migration policy already has been described in the theorem of the previous chapter. It follows from the theorem that the optimal policy can be characterized completely by the Gittins indices. Consequently in analyzing further properties of the optimal policy, we only have to analyze the properties of the Gittins indices.

Primarily we can conclude from the model that there are only *three* indices relevant for the decision maker. More precisely we need to consider only $Z_j(s_j)$ where s_j can take 3 types of states:

$$s_j \longrightarrow w_j \longrightarrow (w_j, \alpha_j)$$

The following Lemma gives useful information concerning the determination of the Gittins indices for our model:

Lemma 1: Given the state of information, (w_j, α_j), then

$$Z_j(w_j, \alpha_j) = \frac{w_j + \alpha_j}{1 - \beta}, \tag{5}$$

b) *Given the state of information (w_j), then $Z_j(w_j)$ is determined by*

$$Z_j(w_j) = \frac{w_j - k_j}{1 - \beta} + \frac{\beta}{1 - \beta} \int \Big(\frac{w_j + \alpha_j}{1 - \beta} - Z_j(w_j) \Big)^+ dG_j(\alpha_j), \tag{6}$$

c) *Given no information about region j, then $Z_j(s_{0j})$ is determined by*

$$Z_j(s_{0j}) = \frac{-c_j}{1-\beta} + \frac{\beta}{1-\beta}\int\Big(w_j - k_j + \beta\int\Big(\frac{w_j + \alpha_j}{1-\beta} - Z_j(s_{0j})\Big)^+ dG_j(\alpha_j) - (1-\beta)Z_j(s_{0j})\Big)^+ dF_j(w_j). \quad (7)$$

Proof: See Appendix

To give a graphical illustration for determining Gittins indices let us denote the right-hand side[9] of equation (6) and (7) by $f_2(k,w,G(\cdot),Z)$ and $f_3(c,k,F(\cdot),G(\cdot),Z)$ respectively. Obviously $f_2(\cdot)$ and $f_3(\cdot)$ are non-increasing in Z. The Gittins indices are determined from the intersection of the graphs of $f_2(\cdot)$ and $f_3(\cdot)$ with the 45° line.

Here we exclude negative Gittins indices from the consideration by implicitly assuming that the support of $F_j(\cdot)$ and $G_j(\cdot)$ is "large enough"[10 11]. More precisely we have to assume for each j

a) $w_j - k_j < \beta\int\Big(\frac{w_j + \alpha_j}{1-\beta}\Big)^+ dG_j(\alpha_j) \qquad \forall w_j \in \text{support } (F_j),$

b) $-c < \frac{\beta}{1-\beta}\int\Big(\frac{w_j - k_j}{1-\beta} + \frac{\beta}{1-\beta}\int\Big(\frac{w_j + \alpha_j}{1-\beta}\Big)^+ dG_j(\alpha)\Big)^+ dF_j(w_j).$

9 For ease of notation we omit the index j whenever it is possible to do so without confusion.

10 The "support" of $F_j(\cdot)$ is defined as the smallest closed set such that there is no probability mass in its complement.

11 Negative Gittins indices would arise if $f_j(\cdot,0) < 0$ or in other words if k_j resp. c_j are "large enough" compared with the support of $F_j(\cdot)$ resp. $G_j(\cdot)$.

Figure 2:

Determination of the Gittins indices according to equation (6) and (7)

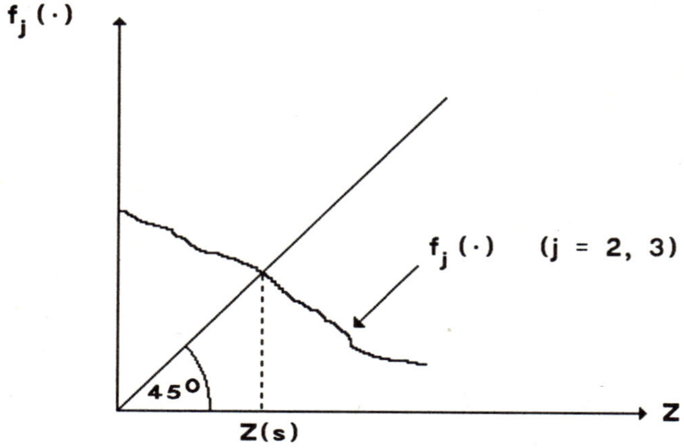

From the definitions of $f_2(\cdot)$ and $f_3(\cdot)$ one can now derive the following conclusions (by shifting the graphs of these functions appropriately).

- $Z_j(s_j)$ is strictly decreasing in c_j respectively k_j, for $s_j \neq (w_j,\alpha_j)$,

- $Z_j(w_j)$ is strictly increasing in w_j.

These conclusions can easily be verfied by shifting the graph of $f_2(\cdot)$ respectivly $f_3(\cdot)$ to the left (for increasing k respectively c) or shifting the graph of $f_2(\cdot)$ to the right (for increasing w). These results seem also to be intuitively plausible. For increasing moving costs respectively search costs should not increase the ranking of a region.

It is more important for the following development to analyze effects on the Gittins indices that are induced by variations of $F_j(\cdot)$ respectively $G_j(\cdot)$. We are mainly interested in varying the distributions with respect to the concept of "mean preserving spread". This is a well-known concept in the "Economics of uncertainty" (see for instance Rothschild and Stiglitz (1971)). Intuitively a probability distribution $F'(\cdot)$ has a larger m.p.s. than $F(\cdot)$ if it has the same expected value and $F'(\cdot)$ can be regarded as construed from $F(\cdot)$ by shifting the mass of $F(\cdot)$ onto the tails. Consequently one can roughly say that $F'(\cdot)$ displays more variability than $F(\cdot)$.

Concerning m.p.s. one can now derive the following result:

Lemma 2: Suppose $F_j'(\cdot)$ and/or $G_j'(\cdot)$ have a larger m.p.s. than $F_j(\cdot)$ respectively $G_j(\cdot)$ and let us denote by $Z_j'(s_{Oj})$ respectively $Z_j(s_{Oj})$ and $Z_j'(w)$ resp. $Z_j(w)$ the respective Gittins indices then we have

$$Z_j'(s_{Oj}) \geq Z_j(s_{Oj})$$

$$Z_j'(w_j) \geq Z_j(w_j).$$

Proof[12]: See Appendix

Remark: It should be noticed here that this result utilizes risk-neutrality of the decision maker which has been assumed so far. Work is in progress where the result ought to be extended to particular classes of risk-averse decision makers.

The interpretation of the above result depends on the economic context which will be elaborated in more detail below. For the moment we should keep in mind the general interpretation that more variability in the wage and/or "quality of life" distribution increases the attractiveness of a region. A plausible explanation for this result is due to the sequential character of the decision process. More variability in the relevant distributions implies more favourable results the decision maker can expect (and naturally more unfavourable results, too). But as the decision maker can revise a

12 The proof is based on the fact that an integral $\int f(x)dF(x)$ increases for convex functions $f(\cdot)$ if $F(\cdot)$ has a larger m.p.s. (e.g. Lippman and McCall (1982)). As the integrands that appear in the integrals of $f_2(\cdot)$, $f_3(\cdot)$ obviously are convex functions (in w resp. α) the graphs of $f_2(\cdot)$ and $f_3(\cdot)$ are shifted to the right as a result of an increasing m.p.s.

decision after results turned out to be bad, more variability may improve his expected pay-off.

Before we apply the results above to rural/urban migration we will derive a further property of the optimal migration policy in the following Lemma. This property connects our model with the well-known job search paradigm (e.g. Lippman and McCall (1976)) and furthermore simplifies the calculation of inbound and outbound migration rates, as will be clear at once.

Lemma 3: *Suppose the migrant knows w_j after a job search process. Then he will stay in region j for at least one further period if $w_j \geq w_j{*}$ where $w_j{*}$ is determined by the equation*

$$k_j = w_j{*} + \beta \int \left(\frac{w_j{*} + \alpha_j}{1 - \beta} - z_j{*} \right)^+ dG_j(\alpha_j) - (1 - \beta) Z_j^* ,$$

where

$$Z_j^* = \max_{i \neq j} Z(s).$$

Remark: Obviously, w_j^* can be interpreted as reservation wage (in the sense of the traditional job search literature) for region j. In contrast to the traditional job search models, $w_j{*}$ depends on many parameters. It also depends on the Gittins indices for the other regions, i.e. it depends on the state of information available about the remaining regions. To summarize our results, we can characterize the structure of the optimal migration policy in our model as follows: Suppose a potential migrant is at the beginning of the decision process. Then he should:

a) calculate the Gittins index for each region and go into the region with the largest index,

b) pay c_j and start a job search process; if $w_j < w_j^*$ search the region with the next highest index, if $w_j \geq w_j^*$ pay k_j and stay at least for another period in this region,

c) after realization of α_j calculate the Gittins index for region j again; if it has become smaller than at least one of the other indices, go into the region with the largest index, otherwise stay in region j.

Now we are prepared to attack the question we put at the beginning of this chapter.

4.2. Rural/urban migration

It has been emphasized by many authors (e.g. Todaro (1969), Harris and Todaro (1970)) that rural/urban migration creates serious problems for the economies of the less developed countries.

Since that time economists worked on different explanations for this phenomenon. Todaro (1969) was the first who gave an explanation in the framework of a microeconomic decision model. According to Todaro, migration from rural to urban regions is attractive if the expected wage in the urban region is sufficiently large. Consequently, a migrant will go into the city even if he might become unemployed (with a given probability).

We will give another explanation below which does not use expected wage differentials at all. For this sake we utilize some ideas of David (1974) and Da Vanzo (1981) who stated that city regions in less developed countries are characterized by two facts:

a) Because of greater heterogeneity of people in the urban regions, there is more variability in the economic facilities and more variability in the quality of life.

b) In general, people have less information about urban regions compared with rural regions.

Naturally, both points are closely related, and we will formalize them by the same mathematical concept. More precisely we will make the following convention:

A region displays more variability in the distributions of w_j *and* α_j *respectively. A potential migrant is said to be less informed about* w_j *and* α_j *iff the mean preserving spread of the distributions of* W_j *and* G_j *increases.*

Concerning the variability of the distributions, this convention is justified by the definition of the mean preserving spread itself. Concerning the degree of information, we can justify the convention by the following reasoning. In the economics of information, one often formalizes the degree of information by the "noise" that is incorporated in a random variable. Consequently, we could say a migrant has become less informed about W_j and A_j if he is confronted with random variables.

$$W_j' \stackrel{d}{=} W_j + X,$$

$$A_j' \stackrel{d}{=} A_j + Y,$$

where $E(X|W_j) = E(Y|A_j) = 0$. Here X and Y can be interpreted as "noise" that has been added to the wage variable W_j and the "quality" variable A_j.

Now it follows from a well-known result (e.g. Rothschild and Stiglitz (1970), Theorem 2) that the distributions of the random variables W_j' and A_j' have a larger m.p.s. connecting the concepts of increasing m.p.s. and decreasing information in a precise way.

By summarizing the reasoning above we can finally explain the following:

Fact 1: Urban regions are more attractive for migration compared with rural regions.

One only has to combine the characterization of urban regions by David and Da Vanzo with the results of Lemma 2. According to the assumptions of our model, we could give more differentiated explanations for fact 1. For the attractiveness of a region might be based on a high m.p.s. of the wage distribution or the "quality" distributions alone or on a high m.p.s. of both distributions. The attractivity might even be generated as a kind of net effect of the m.p.s.'s of $F_j(\cdot)$ and $G_j(\cdot)$. This follows easily from the proof of Lemma 2.

It should be noticed here that our explanation for fact 1 differs completey from Todaro's explanation as the increase in m.p.s. does not change the expected values of the distributions. Consequently, an urban region might become more attractive even though the expected wage is kept on the same level. Closely related to the problem of rural/urban migration is the phenomenon of high in-migration into particular regions strongly correlated with high out-migration (out from these regions). One can observe this phenomenon presumably in urban regions of less developed countries (see for instance Pessino (1987) who analyzes respective data concerning rural/urban migration in Peru). In our view a satisfactory explanation for this strongly empirically supported fact should be based on remigration respectively repeat migration. A consistent explanation for remigration and repeat migration on the other hand can only be given within a sequential migration decision model of the type presented above. We will illustrate this idea by a drastic example below.

In this example everybody is supposed to be identical except for the fact that each individual draws different values of W_j and G_j. Furthermore, it is supposed that the optimization process is done only by people living in the rural region (j=1) and that the parameters of the problem are such that everybody chooses to go into the urban region (j=2) in the first period. In other words we suppose that $Z_1(w_1, \alpha_1)<Z_2(s_{02})$ for every migrant in question[13]. According to Lemma 3, some people who started migration into the urban region will return after the first period as they do not find an acceptable job offer $w_2>w_2^*$. The remaining migrants will stay for at least one further period in the urban region. According to the

13 By considering Z_1 (w_1,α_1), it is implicitly assumed that wage and quality of life in region 1 are already completely known.

Gittins index rule, those migrants will return who have drawn (w_2,α_2) pairs such that $Z_2(w_2,\alpha_2) < Z_1(w_1,\alpha_1)$.

By adding the two sources of remigration we obtain a percentage RM $\left(\overline{F}_2(\cdot), \overline{G}_2(\cdot)\right)$ of return migrants which is given by

$$RM\left(\overline{F}_2(\cdot), \overline{G}_2(\cdot)\right) = \overline{F}_2(w_2*) + \int_{w_2*}^{\infty} \overline{G}_2\left(Z_1(1-\beta) - w_2\right)d\overline{F}_2(w).$$

This number obviously depends on the objectively given distributions $\overline{F}_2(\cdot)$ and $\overline{G}_2(\cdot)$. It is easy to construct examples such that RM$(\cdot)$ is rather large, giving support to

Fact 2: There is a high correlation between in- and out migration.

RM$(\cdot)$ is large for distributions $\overline{F}_2(\cdot)$ and $\overline{G}_2(\cdot)$ which have large mass on their lower tails, that is for distributions with a high probability of low wages and "qualities". This is a phenomenon that often can be observed in urban regions of less developed countries. It follows from the reasoning above that a high correlation between inbound and outbound migrants in our model is actually a high correlation between first-order and return migrants. In extending this example one could think primarily of relaxing the restriction that migrants have only two regions to migrate in their opportunity set. In general, a migrant who is disappointed in a given urban region might prefer to migrate to a different urban region instead of return migration to the rural region. But by taking account of repeat migration the results of our example would become even more drastic.

5. Concluding Remarks

As mentioned, our model could be extended in several directions. For example one could model more realistic information processes such that information about the non-pecuniary returns comes in over several periods whose number is uncertain (with a given subjective probability distribution), or one could think of introducing an explicit formulated job search process that a migrant performs before settling in a region at least for some time, or furthermore, one could think of extending the model such that a potential migrant also takes account of possibly becoming unemployed while living for some periods in the region. Some attempts in this direction have been done in a similar framework by Lippman and McCall (1981). The problem with all these extensions in our framework is the validity of the Gittins index rule which cannot be assured any more. The same assertion is valid for extensions where the saving decisions of a migrant should be incorporated. Doubtlessly, it would be rather important to model saving decisions as they play a major role in the motivation for migration. The authors succeeded in formalizing the saving decision and its economic consequences within a rather simple model where the Gittins index rule is not applicable (Berninghaus and Seifert-Vogt (1988)).

Due to limitation of space we were not able to give a survey over all known applications of our migration model. Here we can refer to Berninghaus and Seifert-Vogt (1987) for applications to international migration especially to guest-worker-migration and to McCall and McCall (1987) where the problem of illegal immigration is formalized as a specialized Multi-armed Bandit problem.

Finally, it should be noted that the MAB model is also appropriate for empirical testing. Migration probabilities can be formalized as probabilities of specific inequalities between Gittins indices which could be estimated by usual maximum likelihood methods. We hope to be able to present some estimation results in a future paper.

Appendix

Proof of Lemma 1: To simplify notation we will use here the following abbreviations

$Z_j(w_j,\alpha_j) \;=\; Z^2$ (we omit the index for the region)

$Z_j(w_j) \;=\; Z^1$

$Z_j(s_o) \;=\; Z^o.$

a) According to (1) and (2) in the text we have

$$\text{(A) } Z^2 = (w + \alpha) + \beta V\big((w,\alpha); Z^2\big).$$

$$\text{(B) } V(w,\alpha) = \max\Big\{Z^2, (w + \alpha) + \beta V\big((w,\alpha); Z^2\big)\Big\}.$$

Inserting (A) into (B) we obtain

$$\text{(C) } V\big((w,\alpha),Z\ \big) = \frac{w + \alpha}{1 - \beta},$$

which implies

$$Z^2 = (w + \alpha) + \frac{\beta}{1 - \beta}(w + \alpha) = \frac{w + \alpha}{1 - \beta}.$$

b) From (A), (B) and (C) we obtain

$$\text{(D) } Z^1 = (w - k) + \beta\int \max\{Z^1, \frac{w + \alpha}{1 - \beta}\}\, dG(\alpha) =$$

$$= (w - k) + \beta Z^1 G\big((1 - \beta)Z^1 - w\big) +$$

$$+ \int_{[(1 - \beta)Z^1 - w]} \Big(\frac{w + \alpha}{1 - \beta}\Big) dG(\alpha) =$$

$$= (w - k) + \beta Z^1 + \beta\int\Big(\frac{w + \alpha}{1 - \beta} - Z^1\Big)^+ dG(\alpha)\ ,$$

which implies the desired result.

c) By taking account of (A), (B) and (C) we obtain

$$Z^o = -c + \beta\int \max\left\{Z^o,(w-k) + \beta\int \max\left\{Z^o, \frac{w+\alpha}{1-\beta}\right\}dG(\alpha)\right\} dF(w).$$

By an analogous reasoning as above, this equation can be transformed as follows:

$$Z^o = -\frac{c}{1-\beta} + \frac{\beta}{1-\beta}\int\Big(w - k + \beta\int \max\left\{Z^o, \frac{w+\alpha}{1-\beta}\right\} dG(\alpha) - Z^o\Big)^+ dF(w).$$

As the integrand can be transformed furthermore into

$$\left\{w - k + \beta Z^o + \beta\int\left(\frac{w+\alpha}{1-\beta} - Z^o\right)^+ dG(\alpha) - Z^o\right\}^+$$

the result follows immediately.

Proof of Lemma 2: As the function

$$g_1(\alpha) := \left(\frac{w+\alpha}{1-\beta} - Z\right)^+ \text{ is convex in } \alpha,$$

and the function

$$g_2(w) := \left(w - k + \beta\int\left(\frac{w+\alpha}{1-\beta} - Z\right)^+ dG(\alpha) - (1-\beta)Z\right)^+$$

is convex in w

it follows from a well-known characterization of m.p.s. (e.g. Lippman and McCall (1982), Theorem 2)) that the graphs of $f_2(\cdot)$ respectively $f_3(\cdot)$ (Figure 1) are shifted to the right with increasing m.p.s. of $F(\cdot)$ and/or $G(\cdot)$ giving the desired result.

Proof of Lemma 3:

Taking account of equation (6) we obtain

$$(*)\ k_j = w_j + \beta\int\left(\frac{w_j + \alpha_j}{1 - \beta} - Z_j(w_j)\right)^+ dG_j(\alpha_j) - (1 - \beta)Z_j(w_j).$$

As the right-hand side of (*) is strictly decreasing in $Z_j(w_j)$, we conclude that (with $Z_j^* = \max Z_i(s_i)$)

$$(**)\ Z_j(w_j) > Z_j^* \text{ iff } k_j < w_j + \beta\int\left(\frac{w_j + \alpha_j}{1 - \beta} - Z_j^+\right)^+ dG_j(\alpha_j) - (1 - \beta)Z_j^* .$$

As the right-hand of the inequality is continuous and strictly increasing in w_j, we obtain the desired result.

References

Berninghaus, S. (1984), **Das "Multi-Armed Bandit"-Paradigma**, A. Hain Meisenheim, Königstein/Ts.

Berninghaus, S. and H.G. Seifert-Vogt (1987), International Migration under Incomplete Information, in: **Schweizerische Zeitschrift für Volkswirtschaft und Statistik**, 2, 199-218.

——— (1988), **Permanent vs. Temporary Migration**, University of Konstanz, Unpublished Manuscript.

Berry, D.A. and B. Fristed (1985), **Bandit Problems**, Chapman & Hall, London/ New York.

Cebula, R.J. (1978), **The Determinants of Human Migration**, Heath Lexington Books.

Da Vanzo, J. (1981), Microeconomic Approaches to Studying Migration Decisions, in: DeJong and Gardner (eds.), **Migration Decision Making**, Pergamon Press, New York, 90-129.

David, P.A. (1974), Fortune, Risk and the Microeconomics of Migration, in: David and Reder (eds.), **Essays in the Honour of M. Abramovitz**, Academic Press, New York.

Gittins, J. (1979), Bandit Processes and Dynamic Allocation Indices, in: **Journal of the Royal Statistical Society (B)**, 41, 148-177.

Gotz, C. and J.J. McCall (1981), Estimation in Sequential Decision-making Models, in: **Economics Letters**, 131-136.

Greenwood, H.J. (1975), Research on Internal Migration in the United States: A Survey, in: **Journal of Economic Literature**, 13, 397-433.

Harris, J.R. and M.P. Todaro (1970), Migration, Unemployment and Development: A Two-Sector Analysis, in: **American Economic Review**, 60, 126-142.

Hart, R. (1975), Inter-Regional Migration: Some Theoretical Considerations (Part 2), in: **Journal of Regional Science**, 15, 289-305.

Langley, P. (1974), The Spatial Allocation of Migrants in England and Wales: 1961-66, in: **Scottish Journal of Political Economy**, 21, 259-277.

Lippman, S.A. and J. McCall (1976), The Economics of Job Search, in: **Economic Inquiry**, 14, 155-189.

Lippman, S.A. and J. McCall (1981), The Economics of Belated Information, in: **International Economic Review**, 21, 135-146.

——— (1982), The Economics of Uncertainty: Selected Topics and Probabilistic Methods, in: Arrow and Intrilligator (eds.), **Handbook of Mathematical Economics,** North-Holland, Amsterdam/New York, 211-284.

Maier, G. (1985), Cumulative Causation and Selectivity in Labour Market Oriented Migration caused by Imperfect Information, in: **Regional Studies**, 19, 231-241.

Mandelbaum, A. (1986), Discrete Multi-armed Bandits and Multi-parameter Processes, in: **Probability Theory and Related Fields**, 71, 129-147.

McCall, J. (1970), Economics of Information and Job Search, in: **Quarterly Journal of Economics**, 84, 113-126.

McCall, J. and B. McCall (1984), **The Economics of Information: A Sequential Model of Capital Mobility**, University of Konstanz, Discussion Paper no. 186, Series A.

——— (1987), A Sequential Study of Migration and Job Search, in: **Journal of Labour Economics**, forthcoming.

Pessino, C. (1987), **Sequential Migration under Incomplete Information: Theory and Evidence**, University of Chicago, Unpublished Manuscript.

Rothschild, M. and J.E. Stiglitz (1970), Increasing Risk: I. A Definition, in: **Journal of Economic Theory**, 2, 225-243.

Sjaastad, L.A. (1962), The Cost and Returns of Human Migration, in: **Journal of Political Economy**, 70, 80-93.

Todaro, M. (1969), A Model of Labour Migration and Urban Unemployment in Less Developed Countries, in: **American Economic Review** , 59, 138-148.

Whittle, P. (1980), Multi-armed Bandits and the Gittins-index, in: **Journal of the Royal Statistical Society (B)**, 42, 143-149.

Migration and International Factor Price Equalization

Gerhard Schmitt-Rink

Abstract: In traditional models of international trade, equalization of factor prices takes place via equalization of commodity prices, i.e. without international trade commodity prices and consequently, factor prices will not be equalized at all. Here it is demonstrated that, all other things being equal, international migration tends to equalize national factor prices and factor shares even in the absence of international trade. Constant rates of net migration tend to equalize national population growth rates, and this in turn tends to equalize national factor prices and factor shares.

1. Introduction

Let us assume two countries 1 and 2 with constant population growth rates n_1 and n_2. Rate n is assumed to differ in the two countries. Constant participation rates in both cases imply a constant growth rate of the labor force. All other economic parameters are assumed to be the same in the two countries, namely, the wage-interest frontier, which represents the alternative sets of labor productivity, capital productivity and consequently capital intensity on the one hand, the alternative constellations of wage rate and interest rate on the other; the average propensity to save (s), and the constant and positive rate of Harrod-neutral technical progress (f), which from period to period shifts the wage-interest frontier w(r) upwards. In both cases equilibrium growth necessitates that capital stock and national income grow at the same constant rate $g=n+f$. Since by definition $g=sx$, where x denotes capital productivity, any growth rate g and savings rate s imply $x=g/s$. A negative growth rate of population and labor force implies a negative equilibrium growth rate of capital stock and national income only if $n<-f$. The borderline between positive and negative economic growth is $n=-f$, not $n=0$.

Since more than one technology, more than one combination of labor productivity and capital productivity are available, the entrepreneurs' choice of technology determines whether equilibrium growth prevails. Under competitive conditions the entrepreneurs' select that technology which at any given real wage rate maximizes the profit rate. Thus any given equilibrium growth rate $g=n+f$ necessitates that magnitude of the real wage rate which causes entrepreneurs to select the technology, which implies $x=g/s$. Obviously the required magnitudes of factor prices and factor productivities do not depend on the sign of the equilibrium growth rate. If the positive equilibrium growth rate g_1 is absolutely equal to the negative growth rate g_2, and if the wage-profit frontier, the savings rate and the rate of technical progress are the same in the two countries, the required magnitudes of capital and labor productivity, wage rate and interest rate are equal, too. In other words: Equilibrium factor prices and factor productivities do not depend upon the sign of the equilibrium growth rate. All other things being equal, the process of economic decline requires the same real structure as that of economic expansion.

Let us assume that in each of the two countries the signs of the growth rate and of the savings rate were the same, i.e. steady-state solutions would exist. Would the competitive mechanism secure stability of the growth process regardless whether the growth rate $g=n+f$ were positive or negative? Obviously not. Assume the real wage rate to be too high (low). Under competitive conditions this causes the entrepreneurs to increase capital intensity at a higher (lower) rate than f, and this would decrease (increase) capital productivity x and therefore the growth rate $g=sx$. These reactions imply stability in the case of positive, instability in the case of negative growth rates. If in the case of negative growth rates the real wage rate is too high (low), the increase (decrease) in the growth rate of capital intensity above (below) the rate of technical progress f implies decreases (increases) of capital productivity. Under a regime of negative growth rates decreases of capital productivity mean increases instead of decreases of the growth rate, and increases of capital productivity imply decreases instead of increases of the growth rate of capital stock and income. In other words: real wage rates above (below) the required level cause reactions which further increase (decrease) the real wage level.

2. Equalization of Population Growth Rates

Let us now consider the economic impact of net migration from country 1 with its comparatively high (positive or negative) growth rate of population and labor force to country 2 with its relatively low (positive or negative) growth rate of population and labor force. One tends to assume that, all other things being equal, net out-migration, since it decreases the growth rate of the labor force, increases capital intensity, labor productivity and wage rate, and that it decreases capital productivity and profit rate, whereas net in-migration, since it increases the growth rate of the labor force, decreases capital intensity, labor productivity and wage rate, and that it increases capital productivity and profit rate. Obviously this is not necessarily true. It holds in the case of positive growth rates, it does not hold in that of negative growth rates of capital stock and income.

Let us assume that all economic parameters are the same in the two countries with the exception of their "own" rates of population growth (which are the rates which would prevail if net migration were zero) and out-migration rates q_1 and q_2, which denote the number of emigrees in t over population size in t-1. Constant own population growth rates n_1 and n_2 determine the growth rates of total population and, participation rates being given, of the labor force N_1 and N_2 in both countries:

$$
\begin{aligned}
N_1^t &= (1 + n_1 - q_1)\, N_1^{t-1} \\
N_2^t &= (1 + n_2 - q_2)\, N_2^{t-1}
\end{aligned}
\qquad (1)
$$

Constant rates n_1, n_2, q_1 and q_2 imply a uniform and constant population growth rate n_0 in both countries and therefore

$$N_1^t = (1 + n_o) N_1^{t-1}$$
$$N_2^t = (1 + n_o) N_2^{t-1} \qquad (2)$$

Solving (1) and (2) for n yields

$$n_o = n_1 - q_1 + q_2 \frac{N_2}{N_1}$$

$$= n_2 - n_1 + q_1 \frac{N_1}{N_2} \qquad (3)$$

Constant rates n_1, n_2, q_1 and q_2 imply a uniform and constant population growth rate in both countries and a constant regional distribution $c = N_2/N_1$ of the total population:

$$c = \frac{N_2}{N_1} = \frac{q_1}{q_2} + (n_o - n_1)\frac{1}{q_2} \qquad (4)$$

If $n_1 = n_2 = n_o$, (4) is reduced to

$$c = \frac{q_1}{q_2}, \qquad (5)$$

regional distribution of the total population is solely determined by the two migration rates. If $n_1 = n_2$, but $q_1 = 0$ or $q_2 = 0$, (3) is reduced to

$$n_o = n_2 - q_2 \quad (q_1 = 0)$$
$$n_o = n_1 - q_1 \quad (q_2 = 0) \qquad (6)$$

and (4) reduced to

$$c = \frac{n_2 - n_1}{q_2} - 1 \qquad (q_1 = 0)$$
$$c = \frac{n_1 - n_2}{q_1} - 1 \qquad (q_2 = 0) \qquad (7)$$

In these cases, where $q_1=0$ or $q_2=0$, (7) determines positive magnitudes, i.e. meaningful results are obtained only if migration takes place from the country with the higher population growth rate to that with the lower rate.

Positive and constant migration rates equalize the growth rates of population and labor force of the two countries regardless whether the own population growth rates are positive or negative. The country whose own population growth rate is larger (smaller) faces a permanent net outflow (net inflow) of people, i.e. the uniform population growth rate. The equalization of national population growth rates via positive and constant migration rates could even change the sign of one of the two country's population growth rates. This could happen if one of the two own rates were positive and the other one negative, whereas the equalized, the uniform population growth rate would be either positive, negative or zero. Any such case of a change from negative to positive or from positive to negative population growth rates implies that the respective country's savings rate is positive or negative according to whether the uniform population growth rate is positive or negative. Otherwise equilibrium growth is not feasible.

3. Equalization of Relative and Absolute Factor Prices

Let us assume that the two countries' own rates have the same sign. Since all other economic parameters are assumed to be equal, the equilibrium growth rates of capital stock and income have the same magnitude and sign. The wage-profit frontier, the growth rate of the labor force, the rate of technical progress and the savings rate being equal, wage rates and interest rates and the shares of wages and interest in national income are equalized, too. Since the savings rate is assumed to be the same in both countries, steady-state implies that capital productivity decreases in country 1 and that it increases in country 2. This in turn means an increase of the real wage rate and a decrease of the interest rate in country 1, a decrease of the real wage rate and an increase of the interest rate in country 2. All other things being equal, migration equalizes the growth rates of population, labor force, capital stock and income, factor prices and shares of wages and interest in national income.

These results, however, do not hold if the two countries' own equilibrium growth rates and consequently the equalized equilibrium growth rate are negative. The own equilibrium growth rates being negative, and all other things being equal, net out-migration decreases instead of increases the equilibrium wage rate, and net in-migration increases instead of decreases the equilibrium wage rate. As in a closed economy, a regime of negative equilibrium growth rates would imply instability. In country 1 the net outflow of labor would necessitate wage decreases, whereas in reality the real wage rate would decrease. In country 2 the net inflow of labor would necessitate wage increases, whereas in reality the real wage rate would decrease. Obviously negative population growth rates which are not balanced by positive rates of technical progress and/or by an inflow of foreign labor would be fatal for the competitive system.

Up to this point, it was assumed that the saving rates were the same in both countries. In this case, migration, in the form described, equalizes the growth rates of population and, all other things being identical, the absolute and relative factor prices in the two countries. Factor price equalization does not occur, as in conventional two-country-two-factor-models, where migration is absent, via trade in commodities, i.e. via the equalization of commodity prices, but through the equalization of the growth rates of the two countries. Equal growth rates, equal savings rates and equal production functions imply the equality of factor prices and factor shares in national income. This does, however, not hold, if the two countries have different saving rates. The equalization of population growth rates via migration could increase as well as decrease the wage and interest differentials, which because of different growth rates prevail in the stage of economic isolation. It all depends on the ratio of the two initial growth rates on the one hand, and on that of the two savings rates on the other. Let country 2 be the net in-migration area, whereas country 1 is the net out-migration area. Under this assumption the following holds:

(1) $n_2 / n_1 < s_2 / s_1$ implies that migration decreases the wage and interest differentials which prevail in the stage of economic isolation.

(2) $n_2 / n_1 > s_2 / s_1$ implies that migration increases the wage and interest differentials which prevail in the stage of economic isolation.

Thus the equalization of the growth rates of the two countries through migration does not necessarily imply the equalization of the factor-price ratios of the two countries. Only in the case where the two savings rates are the same does migration completely abolish the factor-price differences between the two countries.

4. Summary

In this article the impact on equlibrium growth rates, interest rates and wage rates of constant migration rates is discussed within the framework of a two-country-two-factor-model. Constant out-migration rates (the same would hold for in-migration rates) equalize the growth rates of the labor force of the two countries. Wage-interest frontier and propensities to save being given, growth rate equalization implies a decreasing interest rate and an increasing wage rate in the country with the higher natural rate, an increasing interest rate and a decreasing wage rate in the country with the lower natural rate. Interest and wage differentials increase or decrease according to the ratio of relative natural rates to relative propensities to save. Complete factor price equalization implies the very special case of equal propensities to save. Apart from this case unequal factor price ratios provide comparative advantages as the basis for international specialization in commodity production. With differing natural rates, however, no simultaneous steady-state solution would exist. Equalization of the growth rates of the labor force via constant emigration (or immigration) rates thus brings the two countries to the take-off position for balanced expansion with specialized commodity production.

References

Coale, A. (1972), **The Growth and Structure of Human Populations. A Mathematical Investigation**, Princeton.

Feichtinger, G. (1977), **Stationäre und schrumpfende Bevölkerungen. Demographisches Null- und Negativwachstum in Österreich**, Berlin.

Keyfitz, N. (1982), Migration as a Means of Population Control, in: **Population Studies**, 25, 63-72.

Pitchford, d. (1974), **Population in Economic Growth**, Amsterdam. London. New York.

Pollard, J.H. (1973), **Mathematical Models for the Growth of Human Populations**, Cambridge.

Schmitt-Rink, G. (1983), Bevölkerungswachstum und gesamtwirtschaftliche Sparquote, in: Schmitt-Rink, G. (ed.), **Probleme der Bevölkerungsökonomie**, Bochum, 60-70.

——— (1983), Migration und Einkommensverteilung, in: K. Glaubitt, H.B. Schäfer, A. Woll (eds.), **Nationale Entwicklung und internationale Zusammenarbeit – Herausforderung ökonomischer Forschung**, Berlin.

Steinmann, G. (1974), **Bevölkerungswachstum und Wirtschaftsentwicklung. Neoklassische Wachstumsmodelle mit endogenem Bevölkerungswachstum**, Berlin.

Zimmermann, R. (1983), **Demographische Variablen in linearen Produktionsmodellen**, Bochum.

——— (1983), Migration als Mittel der Bevölkerungspolitik, in: G. Schmitt-Rink (ed.), **Probleme der Bevölkerungsökonomie**, Bochum, 71-99.

II. Performance of Migrants

Savings and Remittances:
Guestworkers in West Germany*

Lucie Merkle

Klaus F. Zimmermann

Abstract: The paper presents theoretical and empirical evidence on the determinants of guest-workers' savings and remittances. Using a vast West German data set, it is shown that savings and remittances of migrants can be well explained by remigration plans and economic as well as demographic variables. The empirical results support the theoretical finding that a guest-worker's perceived probability to remigrate affects his aggregate amount of savings negatively. However, the planned future duration of residence in Germany has a significantly negative effect only on remittances.

1. Introduction

The performance of migrants in the labor market is a matter of substantial importance for the immigration and emigration countries as well as for migration policy. It is often conjectured that migrants

---

* SELAPO (Munich), and SELAPO, CES (Munich), CEPR (London) and Humboldt University (Berlin), respectively. Financial support from the German Science Foundation (DFG) is gratefully acknowledged. We wish to thank the DIW, Berlin, especially Dr. G. Wagner for making available the data set used in this study.

work harder and save more because they are positively (self) selected and face a substantial pressure from their home and host countries. For instance, most U.S. cross-section studies have shown that the earnings of immigrants grow rapidly as they assimilate and this growth lead to many immigrants' overtaking the earnings of natives within a period of 10-15 years after immigration (Chiswick, 1978). This view was questioned by Borjas (1985) who used cohort data and found that the across-cohort changes are quite significant. Similarly, Borjas (1987) presented empirical evidence that immigrants in the United States are not necessarily positively selected, as is commonly assumed, but this was again qualified by Jasso and Rosenzweig (1990). Another issue concerns the saving behavior of migrants. It was argued by Galor and Stark (1990) that migrants save more than natives because they almost always face the possibility of return migration.

The purpose of this study is to provide a theoretical and empirical analysis of migrants' saving and remittance behaviour. Remittances can be considered as a special form of savings if there is an intention of return migration, but there are many other motives to remit, like the financial support of relatives. Remittances are an important macroeconomic factor for the emigration country, because they can improve its balance of payments. Unfortunately, there exists no systematic theory of remittance behavior, though there is some empirical evidence on their determinants by Knowles and Anker (1981), Lucas and Stark (1985), and Fox and Stark (1987). We will further elaborate on this problem. We relate both savings in the host country and remittances to a migrant's probability of return migration and empirically test for this relationship using West German household data.

The paper is organized as follows: Section 2 reviews the overlapping generations framework used by Galor and Stark (1990) and summarizes its implications concerning guest-workers' saving behavior. Section 3 explains the data and and discusses basic hypotheses. Section 4 presents the empirical study and Section 5 concludes.

2. Theoretical Framework

To model guest-workers' decisions concerning their desired amount of savings, we proceed along the lines of Galor and Stark (1990) who analyzed the difference in savings between natives and migrants. The overlapping generations model used by Galor and Stark (1990) was initially developed by Diamond (1965), building on earlier work by Samuelson (1958).

Consider a world characterized by an overlapping generations framework in which individuals live for two periods. The market economy is composed of individuals (guest-workers and native borns) and firms. Both act in a perfectly competitive environment within each country. Economic activity is extended over infinite discrete time. In each period, t, a certain amount of a standard consumption bundle is produced, using capital K_t and labor N_t. Suppose that all firms in a country use a constant return technology $Y_t = F(K_t, N_t)$. We assume that $F(\cdot)$ is a net production function which is invariant through time. Output per worker, Y_t/N_t, is given by the production function $y_t = f(k_t)$, where k_t is the capital-labor ratio. The production function is strictly concave and strictly monotonic increasing.

Hence, the first order conditions for profit maximization are

$$f(k_t) - k_t\, f'(k_t) = w_t \tag{1}$$

$$f'(k_t) = r_t. \tag{2}$$

where w_t is the wage rate in units of the standard consumption bundle at time t and r_t is the rental rate of capital at time t. Both, wage rate and rental rate of capital in period t, are taken as given by the firms.

Suppose that in equilibrium the rental rate of capital equals the interest rate in the economy. The interest rate is assumed to be exogenously given ($r_t = r$) due to a highly integrated world capital market (capital is perfectly mobile across countries) and constant marginal rates of return on capital. As a consequence the capital-labor ratio employed in the production of the standard commodity bundle is stationary as well as the wage rate

$$f(k) - k\, f'(k) = w \tag{3}$$

$$f'(k) = r, \tag{4}$$

where k and w are the stationary levels of the capital-labor ratio and the wage rate, respectively.

The firms in an immigration country face the same given interest rate as those in the source country and use the same technology. Wages may differ among countries because of differences in the capital-labor ratio.

As discussed, we assume a simple overlapping generations model in which individuals (migrants or guest-workers and native-borns) live for two periods. The economy consists of two cohorts (the old and the young) at any point in time. People are free to move between different countries. We do not consider a person's childhood explicitly because children make no economically relevant decisions. Each generation consists of migrants (or guest workers) and native-born. In the sequel, only decisions of the first group (migrants) are considered explicitly.

A typical guest-worker lives two periods and is endowed with one unit of productive labor per period. He works in the first period of his life in the host country, and supplies inelastically one unit of labor. At the beginning of the second period, migrants decide whether to return to the native country or to stay in the host country. Second period's labor endowment is then supplied either in the home country or in the host country. Suppose, that the real wage paid to migrants in the host country, w^H, is greater than the wage, w^S, which is available in the native country. Migrants have the possibility to consume only part of their first-period income and save the rest to finance part of their second-period consumption. Savings can be either kept in the host country and/or transfered to the home country (remittances). We do not allow for bequests and other forms of altruism.

Migrants born at time t are characterized by their intertemporal, additive and separable utility function:

$$U(c_{1t}, c_{2t+1}) = u(c_{1t}) + \alpha u(c_{2t+1}) \tag{5}$$

where c_{1t} and c_{2t+1} are first and second period consumption respectively, and α $(0 < \alpha < 1)$ is the future discount factor. The utility function is strictly concave $(u' > 0,\ u'' < 0)$ and satisfies all usual utility properties.

Guest-workers are homogeneous except for one single aspect: at the beginning of period 1 different groups of migrants face a different return probability, p. For example, some guest-workers may plan to stay the first and the second period $(p = 0)$ in the host country, whereas others may intend to return to the source country after one period $(p = 1)$ or may give an equal weight to both possibilities $(p = 0.5)$. For simplicity we take the return probability, p, as exogenous. In reality the return probability of migrants may be influenced by institutional regulations, migrants' demographic characteristics or the migrants' relative depriviation in the home and in the host country. In this context, natives can be viewed as individuals who observe a return probability of zero (see Galor and Stark, 1990).

Consider now migrant i, born at time t. His maximization problem is

$$\text{Max! } u(c^i_{1t}) + \alpha^i u(c^i_{2t+1})$$

subject to

$$c^i_{1t} + s^i_t = w^H \tag{6}$$

$$c^i_{2t+1} = (1 - p^i)\left[w^H + (1 + r)s^i_t\right] + p^i\left[w^S + (1 + r)s^i_t\right], \tag{7}$$

where w^H and w^S is the stationary wage rate received in the host country and in the home country, resprectively, and $w^H > w^S$. The assumption that the wage level in the immigration country is higher than that in the source country, is in correspondance with reality. Underdeveloped countries (where most migrants come from) are often characterized by a very low capital labor ratio. This implies relatively low wages in these countries compared to industrialized ones. r is the exogenously given interest rate paid on savings, which is equal in all countries.

Taking into account the separability of the utility function, u, the first order condition for utility maximization is

$$-u'(w^H - s_t^{i*}) + (1+r)\,\alpha^i\{(1-p^i)\,u'[w^H + (1+r)s_t^{i*}] + \\ + p^i u'[w^S + (1+r)s_t^{i*}]\} = 0. \qquad (8)$$

where $u' = du/ds_t^i$.

Given the assumed properties of the utility function, the optimal value of savings, s_t^{i*}, exists and is uniquely determined. With s_t^{i*} known, the optimal consumption levels in both periods, c_{1t}^{i*} and c_{2t+1}^{i*}, can easily be determined for a given probability of return migration, a given future discount rate, and given wage rates in the host country and the source country.

We now analyze the relationship between a migrant's return probability at the beginning of the first period, p^i, and his optimal amount of saving, s_t^{i*}. According to the life-cycle-theory of consumption and saving, we might expect migrants who have a high propability of remigration to consume abroad less and save more than those with a relatively low return probability (with $w^H > w^S$).

Applying the implicit function theorem to the condition for utility maximization (equation (8)), it can be shown that for $w^H > w^S$, a migrant's optimal amount of savings, s_t^{i*}, is positively related to his probability of remigration, p^i. A formal proof of this relationship is given in Galor and Stark (1990).

The positive relationship between savings and the probability of return migration shows that migrants who observe a high return probability at the beginning of the first period tend to save more than others while being abroad. The return on savings is consumed in the second period, either in the home country or in the host country.

In reality, a migrant's observed return probability is not exogenous. His demographic characteristics, the political and economical circumstances in the migrant's home country as well as institutional regulations (among others) may influence the probability of remigration and hence a migrant's desired amount of savings. In the following section we examine the importance of different factors in determining migrants' savings. Proxies for guest-workers' remigration plans will play a key role in our empirical analysis.

3. Data and hypothesis

In order to study the determinants of migrants' saving and remittance behavior, we utilize data taken from the German Socioeconomic Panel, a large nation-wide survey of households in West Germany. The original data set covers households headed by natives as well as such headed by guest-workers. The sample used for our study consists of a subset of 721 individuals. We concentrated on Turkish, Italian, Greek, Spanish and Yugoslav household heads, who were registered as guest-workers and interviewed in 1988. Only such individuals were kept for which complete information on all relevant variables were available. The data set provides detailed information on migrants' remittances and savings, on their remigration plans as well as on many demographic and economic characteristics.

According to our data set almost all guest-workers, whose total amount of savings is greater than zero, either save while holding a savings account in the host country (Germany) or by transfering money to their home country. At least part of these remittances is saved or invested in the home country while the rest is often needed to support family members. To account for these differences, we use the actual amount of remittances (in German Marks) and the stock of savings, held in the host country Germany as dependent variables. Unfortunately, the individual's amount of savings, held in Germany is coded ordinally in our data set. We are able to deal with this by estimating an ordinal Probit model where we distinguish four different groups of the amount, held on a German savings account (in German Marks) by the guest-worker: 1) no savings, 2) $0 \leq$ savings < 5000, 3) $5000 \leq$ savings < 10000, 4) savings ≥ 10000. The dependent variable remittances is limited to a non-negative range but contains many zeros. For this reason, we have to estimate a Tobit model to deal with this econometric problem adequately. To obtain a better basis for comparisons between the savings and remittances equations, we have coded both variables also in a binary form (1: positive savings or remittances, 0: otherwise) and estimated binary Probit models. Since it is likely that the decision to remit is jointly made with the decision to hold savings, we also estimated a bivariate Probit model.

The probability of return migration is not directly observable but is closely (negatively) related to a guest-worker's planned future duration of residence in Germany. Information on this variable is readily available in our data set. We expect that the amount of remittances and savings are inversely related to a migrant's planned future duration of residence in Germany. Since earnings in the home countries of guest-workers are in general lower than they are in Germany, migrants who plan to remigrate soon perceive a low future income. To smooth their consumption path over the life cycle, they save when staying in Germany. Several other factors may influence savings and remittances. We control for gender (male), marital status (married and never married), household size (number of persons in migrant's household), differences in income (household's net monthly income), the years a guest-worker already lives in Germany, and linear as well as non-linear effects of age (age and age squared). Dummy variables distinguish individuals whose child(ren) live(s) in the home country, individuals whose spouse lives in the home country, individuals who attended university or a job training program in the home country, individuals who attended university or a job-training program in Germany, and individuals who own real estate. The dummy variable which controls for ownership of real estate does not distinguish between that which is owned in the home country and that in Germany. However, according to our data set there are almost no guest-workers who possess houses or land in Germany. So the dummy variable "real estate" controls mainly for effects due to owning houses or land in the home country. Because of the different institutional regulations which apply for Turkish guest-workers and to account for the drastic cultural and religious differences between Turkey and Germany, which are not as severe for most other European countries, we used a dummy variable which takes the value one in case of Turkish migrants and zero otherwise. The descriptive statistics of all variables are given in Table 1.

We expect that guest-workers with relatives (child(ren) or spouse) living in the home country remit more than those who live with their relatives to pay their living expenses. At the same time it is likely that they hold less savings in Germany because they either save or invest in the home country. Household size should have a negative impact on remittances and savings. The household's income is expected to affect savings held in Germany and remittances positively. Since ties to home areas tend to weaken with time, the number of years a guest-worker already resided away from home, is supposed to have a negative impact on remittances and the level of savings. We also expect that Turks have higher savings and especially higher remittances than others because they face more institutional pressure to return to their home country. Further, expectations are that those who own houses or real estate in the home country remit more and may also hold higher savings in Germany. Finally, the effect of age on savings and remittances will likely be non-linear and increasing with age.

4. Empirical Results

The empirical findings are reported in Table 2 and Table 3. Table 2 shows the impact of the independent variables on the amount

Table 1:
Sample Characteristics (N=721)

Variables	Mean	Std. Dev.
Remittances	2773.50	5428.00
Savings	2.25	1.94
Child(ren) live(s) in home country	11.8%	
Number of persons in household	3.83	1.84
Never married	5.8%	
Married	87.1%	
Spouse lives in home country	4.9%	
Age	44.67	10.42
Years migrant resided in Germany	19.28	5.09
Planned future duration of residence	21.08	17.62
Household's income	2971,70	1253.70
Education in host country	11.5%	
Education in home country	41.5%	
Turkish	29.5%	
Owner of real estate	48.8%	
Male	90.2%	

Table 2:
Remittances[a]

Variables	Tobit Estimates	Binary Probit Estimates	Bivariate Probit Estimates
Constant	-29754.0* (4.04)	-4.061* (4.36)	-4.061* (4.20)
Child(ren) live(s) in home country (yes=1)	4267.45* (3.65)	0.668* (3.75)	0.688* (3.66)
Number of persons in household *10	-8140.0* (3.04)	-0.994* (2.72)	-0.994* (2.74)
Never Married (yes=1)	2740.10 (1.04)	0.470 (1.43)	0.470 (1.22)
Married (yes=1)	3034.41 (1.46)	0.491* (1.92)	0.491* (1.65)
Spouse lives in home country (yes=1)	3936.37* (2.20)	0.679* (2.18)	0.679 (1.53)
Age *10	10428.1* (3.15)	1.530* (3.61)	1.530* (3.50)
Age squared $*10^3$	-12386.0* (3.38)	-1.744* (3.72)	-1.744* (3.65)
Years migrant resided in Germany *10	-90.20 (0.09)	-0.105 (0.82)	-0.105 (0.78)
Planned future duration of residence in Germany $*10^2$	-10346.8* (4.47)	-1.327* (4.43)	-1.327* (4.37)
Household's income $*10^4$	10197.4* (2.82)	0.961* (1.99)	0.963* (1.92)
Education in host country (yes=1) *10	-16147.6 (1.16)	-0.372 (0.21)	-0.372 (0.20)
Education in home country (yes=1) $*10^2$	-17905.8 (0.23)	-0.472 (0.04)	-0.472 (0.04)
Turkish (yes=1) *10	16613.8* (1.80)	2.264* (1.81)	2.264* (1.79)
Owner of real estate (yes=1)*10	35642.1* (4.42)	4.880* (4.56)	4.880* (4.46)

Table 2: continued

Variables	Tobit Estimates	Binary Probit Estimates	Bivariate Probit Estimates
Male (yes=1) *10	45798.9*	5.217*	5.217*
	(2.47)	(2.30)	(1.88)
ρ	8588.34[b]	-	-
	(362.50)		
α_1	-	-	-
α_2	-	-	-
AIC	3646.8	435.8	860.09
R^2_{MZ}	0.192	0.303	
(LRT)	(153.2)	(153.68)	
R^2_{VZ}		0.319	

a t-values are given in parentheses. A * indicates significance at least at the 5% level (one-side-test). The correlation coefficient estimated in the bivariate Probit model is $\varepsilon=0.07$ with a t-value of 0.99. AIC is the Akaike information criterion and LRT the likelihood-ratio test statistic. The pseudo-R^2's are explained in the test. The number of observations is 721.

b ρ is the standard error of the Tobit equation, α_1 and α_2 are threshold estimates of the Ordinal Probit, and the standard errors of these estimates are given in parentheses.

remitted and the decision to remit. Table 3 refers to the level of savings held in Germany and the decision to hold a German savings account. As discussed, the decision to remit as well as the decision to hold savings in the host country were analyzed by employing a univariate and a bivariate Probit model. The results of both procedures are shown in columns two and three of the respective table.

The estimated correlation between the probability to remit and the probability to hold a savings account in the bivariate Probit model is very low (0.07) and not significant at the 5% level indicating that there is no efficiency gain in employing this model. This result shows that the univariate Probit models are adequate specifications and that the jointly relevant determinants of the decision to remit and to hold a savings account were included in our model. We therefore concentrate our discussion on the univariate Probit estimates. The pseudo-R^2 measures given are discussed in Veall and Zimmermann (1991), where R^2_{VZ} is based on a normalization of the likelihood-ratio test statistic LRT and R^2_{MZ} is calculated by using individual model predictions of the latent endogenous variable. Both measures mimic reasonably well the OLS-R^2 in Monte Carlo work and indicate a reasonable fit. Also the Akaike information criterion (AIC) is given which is minus the log-likelihood value plus the number of parameters estimated.

Our Tobit estimates (Table 2) show that the amount of remittances is significantly related to ten of the fifteen explanatory variables (at the 5% level). The results are in correspondence with the theoretical expectations. There exists a significantly negative relationship between the amount of remittances and the planned

Table 3:
Savings[a]

Variables	Tobit Estimates	Binary Probit Estimates	Bivariate Probit Estimates
Constant	-1.318*	-1.168	-1.168
	(1.85)	(1.45)	(1.36)
Child(ren) live(s) in home country (yes=1)	0.137	0.224	0.224
	(0.99)	(1.28)	(1.25)
Number of persons in household *10	-0.902*	-0.572	-0.572
	(2.90)	(1.55)	(1.48)
Never Married (yes=1)	0.504*	0.500*	0.500
	(1.88)	(1.67)	(1.60)
Married (yes=1)	0.494*	0.405*	0.405
	(2.27)	(1.71)	(1.61)
Spouse lives in home country (yes=1)	-0.430*	-0.316	-0.316
	(2.01)	(1.25)	(1.19)
Age *10	0.423	0.365	0.365
	(1.28)	(0.98)	(0.89)
Age squared $*10^3$	-0.389	-0.430	-0.430
	(1.10)	(1.05)	(0.94)
Years migrant resided in Germany *10	0.033	0.173	0.173
	(0.33)	(1.37)	(1.39)
Planned future duration of residence in Germany $*10^2$	-0.315	-0.445	-0.445
	(1.25)	(1.49)	(1.48)
Household's income $*10^4$	2.610*	2.884*	2.886*
	(6.87)	(5.34)	(5.61)
Education in host country (yes=1) *10	2.474*	4.387*	4.387*
	(1.65)	(2.34)	(2.35)
Education in home country (yes=1) $*10^2$	-8.021	-0.480	-0.480
	(0.92)	(0.04)	(0.04)
Turkish (yes=1) *10	-1.234	-0.913	-0.913
	(1.19)	(0.74)	(0.73)
Owner of real estate (yes=1)*10	0.272	0.331	0.331
	(0.31)	(0.30)	(0.30)

Table 3: continued

Variables	Tobit Estimates	Binary Probit Estimates	Bivariate Probit Estimates
Male (yes=1) *10	-0.492	-3.246	-3.246
	(0.25)	(1.55)	(1.53)
ρ	-	-	-
α_1	1.212[b]	-	-
	(0.06)		
α_2	1.747[b]	-	-
	(0.07)		
AIC	890.82	425.97	860.09
R^2_{MZ}	0.140	0.137	
(LRT)	(80.26)	(58.72)	
R^2_{VZ}		0.141	

a t-values are given in parentheses. A * indicates significance at least at the 5% level (one-side-test). The correlation coefficient estimated in the bivariate Probit model is ε=0.07 with a t-value of 0.99. AIC is the Akaike information criterion and LRT the likelihood-ratio test statistic. The pseudo-R^2's are explained in the test. The number of observations is 721.

b ρ is the standard error of the Tobit equation, α_1 and α_2 are threshold estimates of the Ordinal Probit, and the standard errors of these estimates are given in parentheses.

future duration of residence in Germany. The estimates also indicate that those guest-workers whose spouse or child(ren) live in the home country, those who own real estate in the home country, and Turkish guest-workers, remit significantly more than others. Also, heads of larger households have significantly less remittances than heads of small households. As expected, a higher income significantly increases the amount of remittances. The amount remitted to the home country increases significantly with age but this increase becomes smaller when the migrant is ageing. Also, male guest-workers transfer significantly more than females. Finally, it has to be noted that neither migrants' education in the home country or in Germany, nor marital status, nor the years away from home have a statistically significant effect on the amount of remittances. As expected, the Tobit estimates of column one differ only marginally from the Probit estimates in columns two and three. Here, a guest-workers planned future duration of residence in Germany has a significantly negative impact on the decision to remit.

The first column of Table 3 shows the estimated impact of the independent variables on the level of savings held on a German account. Only six of fifteen explanatory variables are significantly related to guest-workers' levels of savings. The results also reveal some interesting differences to those obtained in the case of remittances. The key variable planned future duration of residence in Germany has the expected negative sign but is not significant at the 5% level. A spouse residing at the migrant's home country has a significantly negative effect on the level of savings and children living in the home country do not influence guest-workers' savings at all. Furthermore, the results indicate that larger households hold less savings and that guest-workers who have been educated in Germany hold significantly more savings than others. Also married guest-workers as well as those who have never been married have significantly higher savings than divorced or widowed migrants. Household's income has the expected strong positive effect on the level of savings in Germany. Guest-workers' age, gender, nationality, education in the home country, as well as the variable controlling for ownership of real estates, have no significant effect on the level of savings. The binary Probit estimates in the last two columns of Table 3 reveal again only marginal differences. Again the planned future duration of residence in Germany does not influence a migrant's decision to hold savings in Germany.

5. Conclusions

It was studied whether migrants' remigration plans affect their saving and remittance decisions which are important indicators of the performance of guest-workers. Building on earlier work done by Galor and Stark (1990) it was shown that there is a negative relationship between migrants' observed probability of remigration and their savings. Our empirical investigation is based on a sample of guest-workers who lived in West Germany in 1988. We do not observe total savings but the stock of savings held in Germany and the amount of remittances jointly. The probability of return migration should affect both savings in Germany and remittances, whereas remittances also are influenced by the motive to support close relatives in the home country. We proxied the probability of return migration by the individual's planned future duration of residence in Germany. Also other determinants of savings and remittances are considered.

Our findings provide evidence that guest-workers' remigration plans are indeed an important determinant of remittances even if we control for income effects and the possibility that migrants support close relatives who live in the home country. The results which were obtained for migrants' levels of savings held in Germany are less clear cut. The estimated coefficient of planned future duration of residence in Germany is negative, but not significant. It is likely that those guest workers who plan to return early, hold savings mainly in their home country which would explain this finding. With this interpretation, the empirical evidence presented here supports the theory developed by Galor and Stark (1990).

References

Blitz, R.C. (1977), A Benefit-Cost Analysis of Foreign Workers in West-Germany, 1957-1973, in: **Kyklos**, 30, 479-502.

Borjas, G.J. (1985), Assimilation, Changes in Cohort Quality, and the Earnings of Immigrants, in: **Journal of Labor Economics**, 3, 463-489.

Borjas, G.J. (1987), Self-Selection and the Earnings of Immigrants, in: **American Economic Review**, 77, 531-553.

Chiswick, B.R. (1978), The Effect of Americanization on the Earnings of Foreign-born Men, in: **Journal of Political Economy**, 86, 897-921.

Diamond, P.A. (1965), National Debt in a Neoclassical Growth Model, in: **American Economic Review**, 55, 1126-1150.

Djajić, S. (1986), **Migrants in a Guest-Worker System: A Utility-Maximizing Approach**, University of Stockholm, Seminar Paper No. 368.

Fox, M. and O. Stark (1987), **Remittances, Exchange Rates and the Labor Supply of Mexican Migrants in the U.S.**, Harvard University, Discussion Paper No. 33.

Galor, O. and O. Stark (1990), Migrants' Savings, the Probability of Return Migration and Migrants' Performance, in: **International Economic Review**, 31, 463-467.

Guillermina, J. and M.R. Rosenzweig (1990), Self-Selection and the Earnings of Immigrants: Comment, in: **The American Economic Review**, 80, 298-304.

Knowles, J.C. and R. Anker (1981), An Analysis of Income Transfers in a Developing Country, The Case of Kenya, in: **Journal of Development Economics**, Vol. 8, 205-226.

Lucas, R.E.B. and O. Stark (1985), Motivations to Remit: Evidence from Botswana, in: **Journal of Political Economy**, 93, 901-918.

Samuelson, P.A. (1958), An Exact Consumption-Loan Model of Interest with or without the Social Contrivance of Money, in: **Journal of Political Economy**, 66, 467-482.

Veall, M. and K.F. Zimmermann (1991), Pseudo-R^2's in the Ordinal Probit Model, forthcoming in: **Journal of Mathematical Sociology**.

III. Effects of Emigration on the Sending Country

The Impact of International Labor Migration for Turkey

Thomas Straubhaar*

Abstract: Turkey and Yugoslavia remain the only Southern European emigration countries outside the EC. An agreement of 1964 allowing Turkish workers to take up and to exercise an occupation of their own choice anywhere within the EC after December 1st 1986, was checked in the mid-eighties. By German influence and with heavy financial compensation, the Turkish government was pushed to step back from the right of free movement within the Common Labor Market for Turkish workers. This paper discusses some economic consequences of this resignation of the right of free labor movement by the Turkish government. It concludes that emigration only under certain preconditions may influence positively the economy of the sending country. Therefore it is argued that a re-examination of the agreement of 1964 might be in the interest of both the EC and Turkey: The solution of recent migration problems needs the collective action of an internationally coordinated migration policy.

1. Introduction

In the first half of the 1980s Greece (in 1981), Spain and Portugal (in 1986) have become members of the European Community (EC).

---

* Wirtschaftswissenschaftliches Zentrum, Universität Basel, Volkswirtschaftliches Institut, Universität Bern.

Since then, Turkey and Yugoslavia are the remaining Southern European emigration countries not covered by the right of free movement of their labor within the Common Labor Market of the EC (Treaty of Rome 1957, Articles 48 et seq.). For Greek workers the seven-year transitional period had ended at the beginning of 1988 and they have since been allowed to work in any country of their choice in the EC. In the case of Spain and Portugal prior authorization is required up to the end of 1992 for new immigrants seeking wage-earning employment in other EC-countries.

Not so for Turkey. An agreement of 1964 allowing Turkish workers to take up and to exercise an occupation of their own choice anywhere within the EC after December 1, 1986, was checked in the mid-eighties. By German influence and with heavy financial compensation, the Turkish government was pushed to step back from the right of free movement within the Common Labor Market for Turkish workers.

In this paper, I will discuss some economic consequences of this resignation of the right of free labor movement by the Turkish government. I will do so by evaluating the impact from a purely analytical way, free movement of labor might exercise on an economy (section 2) and in broadening the theoretical treatment by formulating a few empirically measurable hypothesis (section 3).

Then, I will indicate some effects, emigration had for Turkey (section 4). While in a former study (Straubhaar (1988)) the quantitative impacts of emigration for Turkey were analyzed, this paper focuses on the quantitative interpretation of these results. It is the aim to demonstrate that emigration only under certain preconditions may influence positively the economy of the sending country.

To conclude, I will argue that a re-examination of the agreement of 1964 might be in the interest of both the EC and Turkey: The solution of recent migration problems needs the collective action of an internationally coordinated migration policy (section 5).

2. The Impact of Emigration for the Country of Origin

In this section, I look at some normative aspects of international labor emigration. Does emigration generate welfare effects for the country of origin? After having presented some basic remarks in the first part of this section (2.1), I examine some of the more recent results of the normative theory of international economics in the following parts of this section (2.2-2.3).

2.1. Some Basic Remarks

In the view of the normative theory of international economics, international labor migration should be mutually beneficial to the participating countries. It is expected that a mobile labor force, migrating from low to high productivity countries allows for a more efficient allocation of the productive factors. As long as the marginal productivity of labor is not equalized internationally, international labor migration provides the participating countries with additional allocational gains by removing relative scarcities.

Such is the basis of the claim of mutual gain from international migration. Three central questions, however, have to be raised:

First: Should we evaluate the consequences of international labor migration from a national or from a domestic perspective?

- From a domestic perspective — embracing only those residing within the country — any costs and benefits accruing to the migrants while abroad do not count for the country of workers' origin.

- From a national perspective - embracing all nationals whether at home or abroad — all costs and benefits accruing to the citizen abroad are considered by the country of emigrants' origin.

Migration, considered harmful (or useful) from a national standpoint, might well be considered differently from a domestic point of view. To illustrate this point, we refer to the example of skill acquisition. The skills acquired by the migrant while working abroad count as "national" benefit only, but they do not count as benefit in a "domestic" view. Seen from a "domestic" perspective the country of origin loses all the possible returns on the investments in the migrant's education without being compensated by the country of migrant's destination. However, once the migrant returns, the (discounted) increase of migrant's productivity due to the skills he obtained abroad is counted as a "domestic" benefit of migration (and a "national" benefit as well).

Second, we have to ask, who receives the gains or losses of migration, and, to what extent is the interest of the migrants the same as the interest of the participating countries? It might be true that some groups may lose while others may benefit from the migration of their national workers. In other words, the distributional effects of international labor migration may diverge from the aggregated national results.

Third, what is the division of the gains between the labor sending and labor receiving country? On one side, referring back to Adam Smith's idea, migration tends to equalize the differences in economic opportunities between the home country and abroad. Formalized in the theory of "unlimited supply of labor" by Sir Arthur W. Lewis, it was thought that, by migration, human resources were being shifted from locations where their social marginal products were assumed to be zero to places where this marginal product was positive.

Therefore, according to this neoclassical theory, international migration of labor should narrow the development gap between the country of emigrants' origin and abroad. From that point of view, emigration is seen as beneficial.

On the opposite side, the Swedish Nobel laureate Gunnar Myrdal and his scholars argue that international labor migration tends to increase the inequality. Formalized in the theory of "cumulative processes" by Myrdal and "backwash or polarization effects" by Hirschman, migration in excess of job opportunities is seen as both a symptom and a contribution to underdevelopment.

Therefore, according to this view, international labor migration harms the economic development of the home country and strengthens the polarization in poor (home) and rich (foreign) countries.

2.2 A Domestic View

When, in the 1950s, economists began to discuss the phenomenon of international labor migration more intensively, there was a diversity of opinions and theoretical analysis on the usefulness of migration (Lewis (1954), Thomas (1958), Galenson and Leibenstein (1955), Ranis and Fei (1961)).

In a first approach to implement the welfare effects of international labor migration into the models of international trade, the MacDougall (1960) - Kemp (1964) model for analyzing international capital mobility was applied to international labor migration by Johnson (1967), Grubel and Scott (1966), and Berry and Soligo (1969). With regard to the welfare effects of emigration Grubel and Scott (1966) argued that under the assumption of perfect competition, emigration should be neutral in its economic impact on the nonmigrants. Given the assumption of their model that an emigrant is paid exactly the value of what he produced, the remaining pie after emigration is exactly the amount previously divided among those left behind. Hence, nobody is better off and nobody is worse off.

This argument is valid only for small magnitudes of emigration. When the effects of nonmarginal migration are considered the conclusion by Grubel and Scott does not hold anymore. Emigration implies that less labor is applied to the same amount of land and capital. Consequently, the productivity of those workers left behind tends to rise and the productivity of land and capital tends to fall. Emigration will be neutral only, if the benefits of the higher wage rates (as implied by the higher labor productivity) offset the loss of the fall in profit rates for land and capital owners (as implied by the lower return on land and capital). Yet, in the MacDougall-Kemp model the gain of workers will not completely offset the loss of capitalists and a "deadweight" loss necessarily occurs (analogous to the "surplus" in the case of an inflow of a factor as analyzed by MacDougall (1960)).

Furthermore, the neutrality of labor migration also relies on the assumption that emigration does not affect the size of the domestic capital stock. Johnson (1967) pointed out, however, that the fate of those left behind depends on the amount of capital the emigrants take with them. Without reference to Johnson (1967), Berry and Soligo (1969) have analyzed the possibility of emigrants moving their assets with them. They showed the different welfare effects depending on the extent to which an emigrant was a "capitalist" compared to those remaining, and depending on the extent to which an emigrant moves his capital with him.

In short, Berry and Soligo (1969) demonstrated that according to the capital an emigrant owns and to the proportion he leaves behind or takes with him, the capital-labor ratio is influenced differently. In the simple neoclassical case (under perfect competition, constant returns to scale and no extern alities) international labor migration lowers the total income of non-emigrants unless the emigrants own a disproportionately high share of total capital (in a comparative static view) or have relatively high wealth-holding propensities (in a stationary dynamic sense) and leave their capital behind them. These results by Grubel and Scott (1966) and Berry and Soligo (1969) have induced a large theoretical analysis of the welfare effects of emigration.

In a more recent paper, Gerking and Mutti (1983) come to the conclusion that under the assumption of internationally mobile capital, emigration of unskilled labor from lower to higher developed countries also provides an incentive for capital to flow in the same direction. "The key behavioral factor is that the greater availability of unskilled labor in the developed country will attract capital out of the less developed country." (Gerking and Mutti (1983), 375)

As a consequence, wage rates are likely to fall in both countries (while the returns to all capital owners rise), and the gap between the wage rates in the two countries may even increase. This result contradicts the conventional economic wisdom that the migration of unskilled labor from less developed countries to higher developed countries should narrow the wage gap between those countries, and therefore reduce the incentive for further migration.

The MacDougall-Kemp model is limited by the fact that it remains within the Heckscher-Ohlin framework. A first approach to overcome this limitation and to extend the model is based on the important contribution by Kenen (1971). In seeking "to identify the welfare implications of net emigration, viewed from the standpoint of the source region or country ... " Kenen ((1971), 238) still remained in the context of the Heckscher-Ohlin model. But his presentation was used by Rivera-Batiz (1982), (1984), and, in a comment by Thompson (1984) who went a step beyond the assumption that all produced goods are tradable. Rivera-Batiz ((1982), 82) examined "the economic effects of emigration on the source country by assuming that there is a non-traded goods sector whose output and price are established endogenously in the economy."

Under the crucial and not very realistic assumption that the economy is originally at a locally stable equilibrium and that the comparative static variations remain in the neighborhood of this equilibrium, they showed that the impact of emigration on the real income of those remaining must be subdivided into its impact on capital-rich (class 1) and labor-rich (class 2) individuals (Rivera-Batiz (1984), 329-330). If emigration consists of individuals with a relatively large fraction of capital — which they take with them — "... the real income of the non-emigrants forming part of the capital-rich class would unambiguously improve, while the impact on the real income of the non-emigrants composing class 2, with relatively larger labor-capital endowments, is ambiguous and may actually decline if the fraction of non-traded goods they consume is small enough." (Rivera-Batiz (1984), 330)[1] In this final evaluation of the impacts of emigration on the country of origin, this approach comes close to the results of the one based on the work by Grubel and Scott (1966) and Berry and Soligo (1969).

A second approach to extend the limitation of the MacDougall-Kemp model analyzes the welfare impacts of international labor migration within a so-called "basic model" (Jones et al. (1986)). This model was pioneered by Ramaswami (1968) and, after being neglected for a longer period, was discussed by a host

---

1 By introducing remittances into the Rivera-Batiz (1982) model, Djajic (1986), 229) showed that emigration need not reduce the welfare of those behind. "If the flow of remittances exceeds a certain critical amount, the remaining residents benefit from migration even if they do not receive any of the remittances themselves." A result that is in sharp contrast with the results of the Rivera-Batiz (1982) model in which the possibility of a gain for the non-migrants is ruled out.

of authors in a special issue of the Journal of International Economics in 1983 (cf. especially the articles by Bhagwati and Srinivasan (1983) and Calvo and Wellisz (1983)).

This basic model is one in which "two countries each produce the same single commodity with identical constant returns to scale technology." (Jones et al. (1986), 313) It is formulated in a way to provide insight into optimal strategy in a world in which simultaneous international mobility of capital and labor is possible.

Originally, the basic model was developed to answer the question whether it might be better for a country to restrict labor migration, allowing capital movements, or to restrict capital movements, allowing labor migration. Ramaswami ((1968), 310) showed that it is better to allow the import of the scarce factor than to export the abundant factor.

Applied to international labor migration, the reason for this asymmetry is as follows: "When a country exports its abundant factor, however, it uses that factor more intensively abroad than at home; and import of the scarce factor eliminates loss on this account." (Ramaswami (1968), 310) Thus, for a labor-abundant country it is preferable to import the scarce factor capital rather than to export the abundant factor labor because emigrants working abroad use relatively less capital (i.e. emigrant labor is used more intensively) than at home, whereas, in the former case, all domestic labor uses capital to the same intensity.

Jones et al. (1986) extended this result, suggesting that optimality requires flows of capital and labor. Applied to a labor-abundant country, this country should allow capital inflow (and tax it) and also stimulate emigration. These results by Jones et al. (1986) are somewhat limited by the assumption that both countries have different factor endowments but share the same technology.[2] Ruffin ((1984), 258-259) showed that productivity differences can either magnify or reverse the results provided by the basic model.

Furthermore, the basic model is restricted to the dimension of one-commodity, two factors. Countries are producing a single identical commodity which renders this model mute for questions concerning the international trade in goods.[3] Adding a third, immobile factor to the basic model, the optimal migration policy becomes dependent upon the country's endowment pattern and the fiscal instruments available to it. "Unlike the basic model, the factor flows which result from a policy of free mobility are now uniquely determined, and sometimes in an unexpected direction." (Kuhn and Wooton (1987), 138)

---

2 This assumption isolates the difference in factor endowment positions as the key characteristic determining the pattern of factor mobility, which parallels in spirit the neglect of inter-country differences in technology in the Heckscher-Ohlin model.

3 The same restriction to a two country, one good, two factor world limits the analysis of international labor migration within a dynamic general equilibrium model, where time preferences differ internationally. Additionally, the conclusion that "in contrast to existing results, unilateral migration immiserizes non-migrants in the immigration country while making non-migrants in the emigration country at least as well off" (Galor 1986,1) is limited by the assumption of internationally immobile capital (cf. Galor (1986,5, footnote 6)). which is one reason for the "... sharp contrast to earlier theoretical results" (Galor (1986), 18).

An extension of the MacDougall-Kemp model to higher dimensions than the one-commodity, two-factors setting of the basic model has been demonstrated by Ruffin (1981). In short, using a model with three factors and two goods, Ruffin (1981) developed results similar to the conclusions of the specific factors model presented above. According to his analysis an increase in supply of one of the (immobile) specific factors, reduces the real reward to the other (immobile) specific factor and increases the real reward of the non-specific (mobile) factor.

Applied to the topic of international labor migration, we could suppose that capital is specific to the industrialized sector and land is specific to the agricultural sector, while labor is non-specific and can be used in both sectors. Commodity prices assumed constant, additional capital (by capital import) would attract labor from the agricultural sector and, hence, reduce agricultural rents and raise wage rates. On the other hand, emigration would decrease the return on both specific factors, land and capital. Again, we may face the problem of how to choose between labor emigration and capital import. The way out of this puzzle can be found by applying the Hamilton/Svensson (1983) results to the Ruffin (1981) analysis: In a situation where capital in the industrial sector and land in the agricultural sector are relatively scarce, and labor is relatively abundant, then it is preferable "... to export the abundant factor, but harmful to import the scarce factor. This is in strong contrast to Ramaswami's result that the scarce factor should be imported." (Hamilton/Svensson (1983), 183)

A generalization of the economic welfare analysis of international migration was presented by Wong (1986). With the help of a new approach to general-equilibrium analysis focusing on the factor markets rather than product markets, Wong extends the Grubel/Scott, Berry/Soligo framework to an m-good, n-factor framework.

In his findings, Wong (1986) derives results similar to those of Grubel and Scott, and Berry and Soligo. Wong assumes that irrespective of the number of goods and factors emigration is detrimental to those left behind in the source country if only one factor can flow.

This result, however, is generally not true if the emigrants take with them a certain amount of physical capital. In that case, "the net effect of the emigration depends on the capital abundance of the emigrants and the amount of physical capital left behind." (Wong 1986), 361)

Emigration is beneficial to those left behind if there is an over all rise in the capital-labor ratio in the economy. "It follows that if both groups of people have the same capital-labor ratio, any finite amount of capital left behind the emigrants will help those left behind." (Wong (1986), 361) A result corresponding to the findings of Berry and Soligo (1969).[4]

The generalized model by Wong allows for a simultaneous treatment of international trade, international capital flows and

---

4 In that context the inverse capital flows also become important. The phenomenon of remittances from the migrants has been neglected in the theory on international labor migration. Lundahl (1985) has analyzed the effects of emigration-cum-remittances on the real incomes of both the emigrants and those who remained behind, and he has derived conditions for gains and losses for each of these groups.

international labor migration, but does not separate into traded and non-traded goods, skilled and unskilled labor force. Nevertheless, extended by the inclusion of non-constant returns to scale and external effects associated with specific factors in the way shown by Ruffin (1981) and Hamilton and Svensson (1983), this model might represent the frontier of research on the welfare effects of international labor migration.

2.3 Conclusions

In a rank-order, from the viewpoint of overall welfare impact, every policy allowing for either trade in goods or international factor mobility is better than autarky (Wong (1983), 241). The welfare effects of a combination of factor movements and goods trade, however, are not necessarily positive. "As is well known, introducing factor trade in a situation with goods trade need not generally be welfare-improving for all countries, since the goods terms of trade may turn against some country which might dominate intra-marginal gains from factor trade." (Svensson (1984), 377).

A sufficient condition for welfare improvement is that the sum of the terms of trade effect (defined as the change in the terms of trade that occurs when factor trade is introduced) and the volume of trade effect (defined as the extent to which the production and consumption distortions associated with any deviation from free trade are exacerbated by the factor movements) is non-negative (Grossman (1984)). In general, no definite conclusion exists about the most beneficial combination of trade in goods, capital mobility and labor migration.

Many approaches were developed to rank-order the welfare effects of simultaneous goods trade, capital mobility and labor emigration. Most of them were based, however, on a perfect market model, assuming that productive factors are paid what their product is worth socially. On the other hand, if the emigrant was paid more than the marginal value of his output, then his departure would increase the average income per capita of those remaining. Additionally, if the emigrant was paid less than the value of his marginal product, then the average income per capita of those remaining will decline. (This underpaying of the marginal product might be especially applicable to higher qualified labor like academic researchers, technical engineers and medical workers (cf. Lucas (1981), 97)).

Under single neoclassical assumptions and under the condition of leaving their capital behind, Berry ((1974), 421) summarizes that "... if emigrants own more capital per person than non-emigrants, gain to the non-emigrants is quite probable and may be substantial; where they own an average amount of capital, gain to the non-emigrants is probable; and where they own a less than an average amount, it is least probable."

The propensity of the emigrants to take their capital with them seems to become a key variable in the evaluation of the effects of international labor migration. It should be said, however, that the empirical measurement of this propensity is rendered difficult by the fact that direct labor migration effects are short term while the indirect effects of labor migration induced capital flows are long term.

Additionally, the long-run economic consequences of international labor migration depend essentially on its impact on the domestic savings rate. Besides the fact that the emigrant's individual savings rate can be higher, equal or smaller than it is for those remaining, the emigration influences the domestic savings rate further. If the emigrant was employed prior to emigration and his replacement is costly or impossible, then his movement is likely to depress profits in the domestic economy. "If the propensity to save out of profit is greater than the propensity to save out of wage income, then the domestic savings rate will decline, having adverse growth consequences." (Stahl (1982), 884)

Finally, emigration of under or unemployed workers eases the pressure on scarce (arable) land for those remaining. Due to the emigration of redundant workers, the land-labor ratio increases, and, consequently, the average productivity and the real income per capita for those remaining will also increase. But two factors may well militate against these benefits (Todaro (1985), 267-268):

- The inflow of remittances may lead to some substitution of leisure for labor with the result that only a small increase in agricultural output, or possibly even a fall, will occur, depending on social custom.[5]

- As long as the present value of the expected income remains higher abroad, there is little reason for potential emigrants to stay at home even if local incomes are rising as a result of

5 This substitution may happen especially in societies where economic activity by women traditionally is seen as undesired. Here, remittances may lead to strengthened restrictions on their participation in the labor force, and to a decline in the economic activity by women.

declining labor pressure. In such a case, the emigration country may swing from the extreme of abundant labor and scarce land to the other extreme of abundant land and scarce labor.

3. Measuring Empirically the Economic Impacts of Emigration

In this section, I translate some aspects of the normative theory of international labor emigration into empirical terms. After some basic remarks in the first part of this section (3.1), I indicate some of the impacts emigration exercises on the economy of the sending country in the following parts of this section (3.2, and 3.3).

3.1. Some Basic Remarks

Translating theory on international labor migration into empirical terms is fraught with difficulties. First, much of the economic theory of international labor migration does not lend itself unambiguously to formal modeling. It is no easy matter to determine how basic theoretical constructs can be formalized in econometric models and measured empirically. Second, the data are rarely available in the detail, extent and form required for anything more than a very superficial statistical analysis. It is for these reasons that to evaluate empirically the consequences of emigration, and to answer the question whether emigration harms or benefits an economy, we carefully have to weigh the different effects discussed in section 2 of this paper and that only a general qualitative interpretation of the results, and not a detailed (quantitative) analysis should be our aim.

To get into the matter more systematically, we have to proceed along three main stages. The first stage is the identification of the relevant effects of emigration, the second stage is the quantification of these effects in monetary terms, and the third stage is discounting the monetary terms to their present values to enable valid comparisons to be made.

For the first stage, we consider two not unrelated approaches to assessing the effects of emigration: "One is to concentrate on particular kinds of migrants — skilled, unskilled and so forth — the emigration of each is than viewed as a project to be subjected to cost-benefit criterion. The other is to concentrate on economy-wide repercussions and assess whether emigration contributes to overall growth and development." (Swamy (1985), 62) With the first approach we run into the problem of whose benefits should be considered, those of the domestic population or the national (i.e. including migrants) population. In addition, such an approach is independent of the magnitude of emigration and, consequently, does not show any indications of the desirable extent of migration. In the second approach, we face the difficulties in defining desirable benefits and undesirable costs. Depending on the focus of interest, migration can be examined using concepts of growth, development, sectoral and regional distribution, or national (in)dependence.

Another question remains: what costs and benefits should be taken into account? According to the project-type cost-benefit approach (most often used in empirical literature) the major benefits of emigration arise from remittances, and from the emigration of unskilled, unemployed workers with no loss of output or investment in human capital along with lessening the pressure in the domestic labor market.[6]

The major costs involve the upbringing, education training and replacement of the emigrating labor force, the loss of production, and the social costs of skilled and professional emigration. Hence, it remains crucial how these costs are measured. Whether an "opportunity cost" (Kindleberger), a "real cost" (Myrdal), or a "government subsidies" (Swamy) approach is used, the costs differ significantly.

In this second stage of the analysis, ideally, the difference is calculated between what happened with migration and expected values in the absence of migration. Conceptual problems and data limitations also cause severe difficulties. Not every migration related event can be measured in (quantitative) monetary terms (e.g. how should we measure in monetary terms the modernization effects exerted by returning migrants on the economic and social environment?). Furthermore, the statistical data to evaluate the benefits and costs of emigration are neither complete nor reliable.

In the third stage, the economic components of present and future streams of costs and benefits have to be discounted to their present value, and summed up. Besides the problem of selecting a

6 In the literature on economic development another benefit of migration can be found. Here, emigration is often seen as a powerful solution to reduce the rate of population growth, potentially enabling an economy to overcome stagnation at low levels of per capita income. In addition to the immediate decline of the population growth rate, emigration may also reduce future birth rates. If the younger and more reproductive members of a country emigrate, a fall in the birth rate will occur.

common valid price unit for aggregating the different issues (foreign exchange, labor and capital costs, savings), the choice of the discount rate and time horizon generate additional difficulties.

3.2 Effects of Emigration

The most obvious effect of the emigration of workers is the relief on the labor market if the emigrant was unemployed. As such it is an inexpensive and simple policy option for countries facing significant levels of unemployment and underemployment. Assuming that emigrants have been unemployed, or if employed are easily replaced, emigration releases these economies from the costs of supporting them and from the (long-run) costs of creating new employment opportunities for them. The emigration of unemployed workers, who consume but do not produce, frees that part of the national income which they consumed for alternative uses.

The emigration of an unemployed worker is a loss of past investment, but it saves the country of origin the current additional investment of scarce resources in people not contributing to the national product. This kind of emigration will leave the national product unchanged, while the average product per capita of the remaining will rise.

The same is true if the migrant was employed but could be replaced by an unemployed person (or by a returning migrant otherwise becoming unemployed at home) of equal skill and knowledge. The costs of adjustment of the unemployed to the specific needs of the new job have to be recognized. These costs are higher the less the knowledge of the new worker corresponds to the required skills.

A great controversy exists about the appropriateness of these expectations on the positive labor market effects of international labor migration. Briefly, the opposite side argues that an increase in the average product of the remaining is hardly probable because "migrants typically do not represent a random sample of the overall population. On the contrary, they tend to be disproportionately young, better educated, less risk-averse, and more achievement-oriented" than the general population in the country of outward-migration (Todaro (1980), 377). Therefore, a high probability exists that these emigrants would have been employed at home and that their marginal product would have been higher than the average product.

Furthermore, because of the imperfect labor markets in the emigration countries, there is limited substitutability among workers of different skill levels. Such labor market segmentation makes it difficult to fill specific vacancies caused by emigration. To the extent that emigrants cannot be fully replaced by unemployed persons (or returning migrants) the average product of the remaining will decline. This loss is even higher when the emigration of highly productive workers leads to a loss of positive external effects, which can destroy the jobs of complementary but less qualified workers who remain at home. As Myrdal ((1956), 94) pointed out, in the long term the emigration of all workers, whether employed or unemployed, skilled or unskilled, is an irrational and very costly policy because "the country of emigration bears the cost of feeding and bringing up generations of emigrants", while the destination country gathers the returns.

Very often it is claimed as a "generally accepted fact" that emigrants acquire some skills and knowledge abroad, at the expense of another country, and that after their return this education could be capitalized to the benefit of the home country. "One hoped-for dynamic gain is the training of industrial workers for the Mediterranean countries in Europe: It is hoped that most will return, and that they will bring back with them skills required for economic development, and also adjustment to industrial life." (Kindleberger (1965), 248)

This argument that returning migrants bring increased human capital with them appears to be questionable. It is based on two critical assumptions (Todaro (1985), 268): "First, it is assumed that emigrants find overseas employment that involves greater skill than they used at home and hence become more skilled. Second, it is assumed that the workers will return home and will be able to apply their new skills domestically."

These assumptions are not a good reflection of reality, and several studies and investigations conducted by the OECD ((1975), (1978), (1979)) show that the facts are quite otherwise. Empirical evidence indicates that jobs open to foreign workers are generally unskilled, offering little opportunity for the acquisition of skills. And if emigrants are successful in acquiring better skills they are "... the least likely to return home, as for them the chance of steady advancement may be better overseas." (Todaro (1985), 268).

The kind of professional skills that the returning migrants acquired abroad rarely suit the production methods and the economic structures of their home economy. Many of the returning migrants return to their previous occupations, move into service industries or remain unemployed, but seldom apply their new skills in industrial activities (see Böhning ((1984), 184-188).

Furthermore, returning migrants, now familiar with sophisticated production techniques, may not wish to work in less capital-intensive industries at home. Rather, many returnees enter the domestic service sector, intending to support themselves with a small vehicle or establishment. "As a result, labor-exporting countries move directly from an agricultural focus to a service-oriented economy, bypassing the development of industrial capacity." (Martin/Richards (1980), 8)

At first, emigration leads to a decline in consumption. If the migrant was employed but at the time of emigration his consumption was higher than its marginal product, the average income per capita of those remaining will shift up. The migrant's overconsumption of private and public goods and services no longer has to be subsidized by the others.

On a static basis, however, it might be that "... foregone consumption by emigrants is likely to be matched almost entirely by increased consumption by those left behind, assuming that output has not declined" (Kindleberger (1965), 242). Therefore, there will be no shift from consumption towards savings in the country of emigrants' origin.

Furthermore, the effects of emigrants' remittances have to be taken into account. It is the purpose for which remittances are used that determines the impact they have on economic activity in the migrants' home countries. If remittances are received primarily by members of the lower income categories, they are probably used mainly to satisfy basic needs. (Remember the operation of Engel's and Schwabe's law.) To the extent that the basic well-being of those remaining in the home country is improved, the use of remittances for such purposes should not be dismissed as simply unproductive (cf. Lutz (1961)). Although it differs in form and intensity from real capital formation, the consumption of basic goods is productive in the sense of human capital formation and, therefore, makes a positive contribution to development.

Furthermore, the construction of a house or the improvement of a house, the introduction of piped water or electricity can result in a remarkable improvement in the quality of life for the emigrants' family. The same can be said with regard to the purchase of durable consumer goods.[7]

Remittances of emigrants' savings from income earned abroad are an important element in the balance of payments of their home countries. They offset the often chronic balance of payments

---

[7] Moreover, remittances-induced expenditures generate a multiplier process which will lead to an increase in aggregate demand well in excess of the original extent of the remittances. Giving no more than a rough idea of orders of magnitude, Abdel-Fadil (1985,22) obtained for construction workers in the case of Egypt a multiplier of 2.5 to 3 (assuming zero substitution of remittances for domestic income), and 2 to 3, respectively (if a substitution of remittances for domestic income in the amount of 20% is taken into account). Choucri/Lahiri ((1983), 17-18) in their study on "the macroeconomic impacts of remittances in Egypt" calculated a multiplier of the order of 1.26 for light industry and 2.8 for aggregate real value added with respect to change in real investment demand induced by increased workers' remittances.

deficits, reducing the shortage of foreign exchange. The often crucial restraint imposed on the economic development of the migrants' home countries by balance of payments deficits can be eased, thanks to remittances. As they bear no interest, do not have to be repaid, and their use is not tied to particular investment projects with a high import content, they have a more positive impact on the balance of payments than other monetary inflows (such as direct investments or loans) which would have the same effect in purely accounting terms.

This obvious and easily measured positive balance of payments effect of remittances was quickly recognized and measures were taken to increase such inflows of foreign exchange.[8]

In fact, the effects of migrants' remittances on their home countries have to be analyzed further than only by the extent the remittances finance the import of commodities or compensate for trade balance deficits, or to the extent they increase the average national income. Apart from the obvious positive balance of payments effect, which is easy to detect empirically (Straubhaar (1983)), they have an impact on economic activity in the home

8 To give only a short survey about the most important measurements to attract and increase the flows of remittances, we mention: Foreign Currency Accounts with preferential conditions (like special foreign exchange and interest rates), preferential housing schemes (like special loans and housing saving arrangements), tax relief or relaxation (on import duties and investment taxes), and information services (on potential investment projects). (For a more detailed description cf. Cases Mendez and Cabezas Moro (1976), Van Gendt (1977), Rogers (1981) and Straubhaar (1983). The balance of payments effect of remittances is described at length in Straubhaar (1983, 1985).)

country. Depending on how they are spent (to purchase durable or non-durable consumer goods, essentials or non-essentials, home produced or imported goods) or invested, their effects on production, inflation and imports are different.

A crucial factor is the extent to which the additional demand induced by remittances can be met by expanding domestic output. The flexibility with which domestic supply reacts to the extra demand will determine whether remittances will have positive employment effects or adverse inflation effects and whether additional imports will be necessary.

Furthermore, remittances might induce the postponement or neglect of restructuring the production processes in the emigrants' home countries. Thanks to remittances, there is no urgent need to resolve the employment and productivity problems, which might have been reducing the international competitiveness of the emigration countries on the goods market. However, the procurement of foreign exchange by the short term expedient of exporting labor instead of goods does not relieve an economy of the long term need to finance imports of goods and services out of export earnings.

Moreover, emigrants' remittances are an uncertain source of foreign exchange. They fluctuate not only with short term labor demands of the immigration countries, but also with the saving/investment/remittance-decisions of the emigrants. These short term factors may well work against the long term economic development process.

In the long term, the consequences of emigration depend on the adjustment elasticity of the domestic economy. The more (less) elastically an economy reacts in relation to the consequences of the emigration of labor, the more likely is emigration to help (hurt) the economic development of the emigrants' home country.

At first the emigration of workers affects the capital-labor ratio according to the capital they own and to the proportion they leave behind or take with them. If labor emigration raises the capital-labor ratio, the productivity of labor increases and capital productivity declines. But in a longer term the domestic economy may move its production away from labor-intensive output toward capital-intensive output. This change in the production process might be smaller, equal or greater than the initial emigration-related change.

The long-run economic consequences of international labor migration also depend essentially on the impact of emigration on the domestic savings rate. According to the emigrants' individual savings rates and to the propensity to save out of capital income and wage income, the domestic savings rate declines, having adverse growth consequences (cf. Stahl (1982), 884). Moreover, emigration of under- or unemployed workers eases the pressure on scarce arable land for those remaining. The emigration of redundant workers increases the land-labor ratio, and, consequently, the average productivity and the real income per capita for those remaining.

Finally, another long term consequence concerns the effects of emigration on the international division of labor between the groups of emigrants' home and destination countries. Without access to foreign labor, many of the relatively labor-intensive industries in the destination countries would have faced a labor shortage. Correspondingly, increasing wages would have forced them to reallocate their labor-intensive firms to the countries of emigrants' origin.

The alternatives, "production in the lower wage countries of emigrants' origin" and "trade in place of migration", would have become more attractive (Hiemenz and Schatz (1979)). Inverse capital flows might have provided more employment opportunities to the collective labor force of the countries of emigrants' origin than might have been created by emigration flows. In other words, by emigration the countries of origin may gain individually but lose collectively.

3.3 Conclusions

The economic consequences of emigration remain a matter of substantial controversy and conflicting hypotheses. To summarize the descriptive presentation of this section, we state the expectations of the outcome of emigration for the country of workers' origin:

Hypothesis 1: If the emigrant has been unemployed, then his emigration will increase the average real income per capita of those remaining.

Hypothesis 2: If the emigrant has been employed, than his emigration may increase, not influence, or decrease the average real income per capita of those remaining, depending on how much has been paid for the marginal product of the emigrant.

Hypothesis 3: If the emigrant has been employed, and was paid a wage higher (equal, smaller) than the value of his marginal product, then his emigration may decrease (not influence, increase) the average real income per capita of those remaining.

Hypothesis 4: If the emigrant was a "capitalist" (compared to those remaining), then his emigration may increase, not influence, or decrease the average real income per capita of those remaining, depending on the proportion of the capital he takes with him relative to the average amount of capital per head of the non-emigrants.

Hypothesis 5: If the emigrant left his capital at his place of origin, the capital-labor ratio is always positively affected.

Hypothesis 6: If the emigrant owned more (the same or less) capital than the non-emigrants, but has taken his assets with him, the influence on the capital-labor ratio is negative (neutral or positive).

Hypothesis 7: If the emigrant's marginal product was higher (smaller) than the average product, his emigration lowers (raises) the average output per capita of the non-emigrants (but not necessarily their average income per capita; cf. hypothesis 3).

Hypothesis 8: If the emigrant was employed, the less he can be replaced by an unemployed person and the higher the adjustment costs, the more his emigration lowers the average income per capita of the non-emigrants.

Hypothesis 9: If the emigrant was employed, the more his work was complementary to other production factors the more his emigration lowers the average product per capita of the non-emigrants.

Hypothesis 10: If an emigrant has paid more (less) taxes than he has consumed public goods and services, his emigration decreases (increases) the average availability per capita of public goods and services for the non-emigrants.

Hypothesis 11: If there are economies of scale in the provision of public goods and services, emigration increases the average cost per capita of public goods and services for the non-emigrants.

Hypothesis 12: If an emigrant had a higher (equal, smaller) propensity to save than the non-emigrants, his emigration decreases (does not influence, increases) the average income per capita of the non-emigrants, in the long run (abstracting from the possible inflow of remittances and savings).

Hypothesis 13: If an emigrant was employed, and his replacement is costly (or impossible), his emigration is likely to depress profits in the country of origin, stimulating firms to invest in labor-saving technologies, and, consequently, reducing the labor absorptive capacity of the industry.

Hypothesis 14: If an emigrant is younger, more qualified, higher skilled, better educated and more dynamic than the average non-emigrant, his emigration decreases the chances for economic development and cultural change in the country of his origin.

Hypothesis 15: If an emigrant acquires human capital abroad (at the expense of the destination country), the more efficiently he can use his additional skills after his return the more beneficial is his return for his country of origin.

While the formulation of these theoretical hypotheses is fairly non-controversial, whether emigration helps or harms a country depends on empirical analysis in an appropriate econometric model. We should not expect generally valid answers in every case. The empirical results may well differ according to the nation-specific characteristics and economic performance of the various emigration countries.

4. The Impact of Emigration for Turkey

In this section, I look at the impact emigration had for the Turkish economy. First, I shortly present some characteristic facts of the Turkish emigration flows (section 4.1). Then, I examine the quantitative effects of emigration, but will concentrate at the qualitative interpretation of these impacts.

4.1 Emigration Flows from Turkey

Emigration is a rather recent phenomenon in the case of Turkey, and has no colonial roots. Before 1960, officially tolerated emigration from Turkey did not take place and Turkish workers could emigrate only with a tourist visa. A migration policy to control emigration on the basis of bilateral treaties became valid after 1960.

Turkey began to export labor on a significant scale after the negotiation of an official agreement with Germany in 1961. In the first period between 1964 and 1966 about 55,000 people left Turkey annually for Northern Europe. The emigration of Turks dropped to about 15,000 in 1967 due to the economic recession of 1967 in Germany. After an increase to 60,000 people in 1968, Turkish labor emigration grew to an unprecedented extent from 1969 to 1973, and about 115,000 people per year left Turkey for Northern Europe.

At the end of this period of massive labor emigration to Northern Europe, the stock of Turkish workers in the EC destination countries had greatly increased. In 1972, Germany employed about half a million Turkish workers (= 85% of all Turkish emigrants), the Netherlands employed about 30,000 (=5%), France 20,000 (=3%) and Belgium 15,000 (=2%) Turkish workers. The total number of legally employed Turkish workers in the EC destination countries amounted to about 700,000 people in 1974 (Penninx 1982,787). The emigration flows from Turkey were characterized by the following facts (cf. Paine 1974):

- Male: 85% to 95% of the emigrants were male.
- Rich area of origin: "The richer, more westernized and more conveniently located regions of Thrace and Marmara, and North Central Anatolia have had a dominant share throughout, not just absolutely but also relatively, in the sense that their share in supplying migrants greatly exceeds their share in the total population." (Paine 1974,72) . Young: "As would be expected, migrant workers have been concentrated in the 20-45 years old age group, ..., the proportion of migrant

workers in the younger age groups is substantially higher than that for the indigenous economically active population ..." (Paine 1974,76).

- Married: 82% of the Turks in Germany were married but less than half of the male Turks had their wives with them.
- Literate: "The proportion of literates among Turkish migrants has been substantially higher than that for the indigenous population." (Paine 1974, 79)
- Educated and skilled: The educational levels of Turkish emigrants exceeded those of the remaining Turks, especially for women. There was also no doubt that the emigrants were relatively highly-skilled as compared with the non-emigrating Turks (Paine 1974, 80-81). – Employed: In 1963, only 4% of the total emigrants and 3% of the male emigrants had been unemployed at the time of application for emigration permission.

After 1973 when the Western European economies were shocked by the oil price increase and the following recession, they took steps to restrict immigration almost completely. Consequently, Turkish emigration to Western Europe and to Germany especially stopped and the official and legal emigration flows dropped to a few hundred workers per year. Instead, the illegal migration flows and the number of refugees and asylum seekers increased greatly in the second half of the 1970s, and in the 1980s. The more legal migration flows from Turkey to the Western European immigration countries became restricted, the more Turkish people tried to enter the destination countries as refugees or asylum seekers.[9]

For the second half of the 1980s, official figures (i.e. those of the placement services of the Turkish Labor authorities) show that the major part of the recorded emigration goes to the Near East and to North Africa (i.e. 98%; OECD SOPEMI (1989)). In 1987, about 40,000 Turks emigrated, two thirds (27,000) of them to Saudi Arabia, and a quarter (11,000) to Libya (OECD SOPEMI (1989)).

About 70% of the emigrants were qualified workers like skilled building tradesmen (carpenters, bricklayers, plasterers), mechanics and other engineering workers (smiths, welders, etc.), drivers and electricians.

By origin, the areas bordering to the Sea of Marmora and Central Anatolia provided most of the official emigration in the 1980s followed by the Black Sea and Aegean coasts with the Mediterranean coast and the Eastern and South-Eastern areas some way behind.

The total Turkish population resident abroad in 1987 is estimated at 2.35 million people. About 90% of them live in Western Europe, 6.5% in the Near East and North Africa and 3.5% in Australia. 70% of the Turkish population resident abroad in 1987 is in Germany, 8.7% in France, and 7.6% in the Netherlands (all data from OECD SOPEMI (1989)).

---

9 According to the OECD SOPEMI (1988) data about 50,000 Turkish people per year entered Germany as asylum seekers in the years 1980 to 1987.

4.2 Quantitative Impacts of Emigration for Turkey

Based on the hypotheses formulated in section 3.3 we may analyze some of the effects of labor migration for Turkey. Due to the absence of reliable and complete data to compute the discounted present value of all expected costs and benefits of emigration, and due to the conceptual problems of aggregating the individual items to a net balance, first, I discuss some of the consequences in a piecemeal manner, refraining from trying to sum up the partial findings. The empirical results for Turkey can be summarized as follows (Straubhaar (1988)):

In the 1960s, emigration alleviated to a small part only the unemployment problems of the Turkish labor surplus, and it only lightly reduced the social costs associated with unemployment. After unilateral actions to close their frontiers had been taken by the receiving countries between 1973 and 1975, Turkey lost this outlet for its labor surplus. Additionally, it was confronted with returning migrants who had to be reinserted into an already slack domestic economy.

Unlike the Northern European immigration countries, Turkey had no control over massive return migration flows, and over the serious potential problems they could create. Moreover, the idea that the returning migrants accumulated human capital while working abroad that could have been made available for domestic development, has often not lived up to initial expectations.

With regard to the effects of remittances for the Turkish economy, we may suggest the following conclusions:

- The nominal data on remittances greatly overestimate their real value; the difference between nominal and real average growth rates for the period from 1960 to 1981 amounts to between 30% and 40%.

- Remittances have a significant impact on gross domestic product in the magnitude of around 5-10% only in Turkish regions below a certain level of development. The more advanced the economy, however, the less marked the effect of remittances are.

- The increase in the demand for consumer goods induced by remittances had positive output effects in the sixties and negative inflation effects at the end of the seventies. However, these effects tend to be overestimated for the economy as a whole and underestimated for individual regions or sectors.

- Remittances increased potential savings by an average of only about 3% in Turkey. These savings were used only seldom to purchase "productive" capital goods.

- Remittances ranged to around two-fifths of the value of merchandise exports, and the average proportion of deficits in the trade account covered by remittances ranged to 60-80% between 1960 and 1981.

- The "boomerang hypothesis" that remittances greatly increase the demand for imports and therefore flow back abroad without affecting the domestic economy is not substantiated. Only a small proportion of about 2% was used directly to purchase foreign goods. The overwhelming majority remained within the economy as additional potential demand for domestic goods.

Altogether, I conclude that the expected effects of emigration for the Turkish economy are miscalculated in many cases. There was a tendency to overestimate the benefits and to underestimate the costs of emigration. The impact of remittances on the economies of migrants' home countries often adduced to legitimize emigration have probably been grossly overestimated. The undeniably positive balance of payments effect and the positive but often weak output effect were partly offset by adverse inflation effects.

The result that emigration had a positive but rather weak impact for the Turkish economy are confirmed by the outcome of a simultaneous-equations migration model (Straubhaar (1988), 212). According to the empirical results by a simulation exercise of the model under the assumption of no emigration in Turkey the real income per capita would have been smaller, while the unemployment rate might not have changed much.

4.3 Conclusions

The empirical experience of the migration flows from Turkey to Germany calls into question the expected benefits of emigration promised by the normative theory of international economics. Emigration was a process selective to sex, age, and productivity. It attracted men rather than women, younger people rather than adults, and more highly educated, more strongly motivated, and more experienced workers rather than unskilled and unemployed labor forces. With regard to the gain of human capital by the vocational skills acquired abroad, the picture is equally bleak: Remigration was as selective as emigration, and it was largely the unsuccessful migrant unable to become integrated in the society of reception who returned to Turkey.

Emigration was not the safety valve for the Turkish labor surplus. It was an efficient but weak policy solving the problems of domestic unemployment only for a limited period, based on the willingness of the immigration countries to accept migrant workers. Once the Northern European immigration countries (i.e. Germany) had taken unilateral action to almost completely close their borders to the immigrating Turkish labor force, the migration-based labor market policy caused the domestic labor market to depend on foreign demand not only for goods but also for labor.

Remittances were an important source of foreign exchange for Turkey, enabling it to stabilize its balance of payments. On the other hand, remittances had a significant impact on gross domestic product only in regions below a certain level of development. The increase in the demand for consumer goods induced by remittances had positive output effects in the sixties and negative inflation effects at the end of the seventies.

Remittances created additional purchasing power in Turkey, which on one hand increased the average standard of living in many cases. On the other hand, they did not necessarily lead to the development goals of sustained capital investment, increased productivity, and job expansion. Rather, it seems that the more reliant on remittances the Turkish economy became the more vulnerable and dependent on the immigration policy of the Northern European countries it was. Once the immigration countries closed their borders, the Turkish economy not only had to absorb a substantial number of returning workers, but it also faced a problem of only moderate growth of remittances.

On an aggregated national level, emigration was a weak economic power and its overall effects are rather marginal. Cautiously interpreted, the quantitative findings indicate no empirical evidence that international labor migration harmed the overall economic development of the Turkish economy. Furthermore, the simulation exercise suggest a positive contribution of emigration to the overall economic growth of the Turkish economy. These results, however, neither were intended nor do they allow for a definitive evaluation of the consequences of international labor migration for Turkey. The paucity of a large set of reliable, relevant data at an appropriate level of detail makes it impossible to develop and test formal econometric models of high complexity. The findings do not reflect the regional selectivity of migration which occurs at all levels and arises out of a complex set of technical, historical, economic, social and cultural factors. The economically less developed regions (Anatolia) were the main source of emigration. In these regions the macroeconomic indicators of economic and social development clearly indicate that the initial inequality was not eliminated, despite the massive emigration. On the contrary, the initial inequality has increased during the decade of large emigration.

5. The Need for Collective Action

In this section, I broaden the discussion of the impacts of emigration for Turkey by some basic remarks (section 5.1). Afterwards, I will indicate that contemporary international labor migration is characterized by a legal asymmetry (section 5.2) that calls for collective action in the interest of both the countries of emigration and the countries of immigration as well (section 5.3).

5.1 Some Basic Remarks

In general, the evaluation of the impacts of emigration is still a subject of considerable controversy, and economic analysis is unclear whether emigration helps or harms the country of workers' origin. This dispute is an old one: In the mercantilist era, with certain exceptions, emigration was regarded as harmful, weakening the efforts to achieve a large population. When the classical economists theorized international trade, they had not much to say about international migration.[10] In their static doctrine of comparative costs, free trade was a complete substitute for international labor migration, and there was no need for movements of factors between countries.

Once the classical assumption of internationally immobile labor was dropped, a controversial debate began about the economic effects of international labor migration. On one side, emigration was regarded as a human capital export, inappropriate for the

[10] This statement is not true for the case of colonization. Within the "art of colonization", emigration from the mother country to the colony was broadly discussed; for an overview cf. Thomas ((1973), chapter 1).

development of the countries of workers' origin. According to this view emigrants are raised to adulthood, fed and educated for years only to lose the return in their productive years. On the other side, the benefits of emigration were emphasized. That is to say: The large pool of unskilled surplus labor could be reduced, remittances were received, and, over the long run, economic development might be stimulated as migrants return with additional skills and adjustment to modern industrial life.

By analyzing the case of the Turkish economy, I suggest that the consequences of emigration depended on the level of economic development of the sending countries. They were particularly helpful in the first stage of economic development.

In the early days of mass emigration from Turkey to Northern Europe when Turkey was about to take off on the first stage of its economic development, emigration reduced labor surplus, thus helping to lesson labor market tensions. Furthermore, remittances had a direct influence on development. They facilitated larger imports of goods and equipment which were essential in these early stages of economic growth, stimulated domestic demand and increased the low level of available income for basic needs.

Once, however, the first stage of economic development is passed, the positive effects of emigration on the home economy decreases. The selectivity of the migration process deprived the Turkish economy of a skilled, dynamic and relatively highly productive labor force. Additionally, the remittances stimulated demand and fueled domestic inflation.

Consequently, I suggest that Turkey and the other Southern European sending countries miscalculated the expected effects of emigration in many cases. They tended to overestimate the benefits and to underestimate the costs of emigration. The impact of remittances on the economies of migrants' home countries, often used to legitimize an emigration stimulating policy, has probably been grossly overestimated. The undeniably positive balance of payments effect and the positive, but often weak, output effect were partly offset by adverse inflation effects.

It became increasingly obvious that emigration was the consequence and not the cause of the lower level of development in Turkey and the other sending economies. Emigration has not solved the basic problems of lower development neither in Turkey nor in the other Southern European sending countries. It eliminated a minimal part of the labor surplus but did not in itself generate efficient impulses to overcome the causes of their structural labor market difficulties.

To solve these basic problems of economic development, a policy directed against the causes of the weak economic performance is more powerful than a policy that stimulates emigration. Emigration scratches the surface of the structural problems but hardly activates a mechanism for self-sustained development in the long run.

5.2 The Legal Asymmetry of International Labor Migration

The phenomenon of international (labor) migration is characterized by a legal asymmetry. In general, a country of origin is denied the right to close its borders to bonafide emigrants by the Universal Declaration of Human Rights. However, a country of immigration has the undisputed right to decide whom and how many people it admits.[11]

Within such an institutional framework, granting the right of free emigration and restricting the right of immigration, the country of origin has almost no possibility to control the emigration flows according to its interest, while the country of destination can close its borders when immigration is felt to be a national disadvantage.

Basically, an immigration control system becomes established or more restrictive in times when the social costs of the immigrants are rising and their economic benefits are declining. In slightly more detail, at least four different economic determinants can be seen as explanations of (more restrictive) immigration control systems (for a detailed presentation cf. OECD (1979), 21-23)):

- First, minimizing unemployment among the domestic labor force by "exporting" rising unemployment to the greatest possible extent in the form of a migrant labor force.
- Second, minimizing the costs of growing social tension created by the presence of a large foreign labor force.
- Third, reducing the dependency on, and the social welfare costs of, a foreign labor force.

---

11 Of course, the right to "leave any country, including his own" is not granted all over the globe. Many countries enforce more or less strict (re-)emigration regulations. Weiner ((1985), 444-445) specifies five sets of exit rules: Prohibition Exit Rules, Selective Exit Rules, Permissive Exit Rules, Promotional Exit Rules and Expulsion Exit Rules.

- Fourth, adjusting the national policy to the migration policies of other immigration countries, avoiding being the last open port and becoming flooded with immigrants.

The strength of the immigration control systems may depend on both economic and non-economic principles.[12] Weiner (1985), 444) suggests five different degrees of rules of entry: i) Promotional Entry Rules, ii) Unrestricted Entry Rules, iii) Selective Entry Rules, iv) Unwanted Entry Rules, and v) Prohibitive Entry Rules.

In general, we would expect that the higher the substitutability of foreign for domestic workers, the more restrictive are the restrictions to immigration. It is where an increase in immigration would cause a decline in the domestic labor forces' wages or, if their wages are inflexible, would lead to an increase in their unemployment.

5.3 Conclusions

While this paper is not the place to discuss the problems mass migration flows create for the Nothern European countries of immigration, the remarks presented in this section made it obvious that the immigration control systems of the EC-destination

---

[12] In the following, I am looking at the economic causes of the immigration control systems only. I neglect, therefore, moral-philosophical terms (Why do nation states feel they can exclude others from their borders? For an answer based on the disregard of the cosmopolitan Pareto-optimality, the single-planetary-rights, and the natural rights as well cf. Bhagwati ((1984), 680-681)), and ethnic preferences of societies (based on racist prejudice).

countries have closely followed economic lines, drawn by the domestic demand for labor. The strictness of the immigration restrictions seemed to be inversely related to the domestic labor surplus. The higher the unemployment rate in the EC-destination countries (and the more restrictive, therefore, their immigration control system) the less immigrants have been admitted (and the more foreign workers have been sent back). Immigration became a privilege rather than a right, and the Northern European destination countries controlled the demand of foreign labor in a highly selective way, according to their needs. Moreover, the Northern European countries stimulated the return of migrants, confronting the emigration countries with additional workers who had to be reinserted into an already slack domestic economy.

On the other hand, the emigration countries have no possibilities to control their emigration flows. Emigration is viewed as a human right and the emigration countries are in no position to regulate the supply of manpower on the international labor market.

These two results combined, I suggest that strong migration flows neither are in the interest of the immigration countries nor in the interest of the emigration countries. Consequently, the solution of recent migration problems indicates the need for collective action within an internationally coordinated migration policy.

Such a policy should be in the focus of both immigration and emigration countries. Hereby, the regulation of free movement of labor within the EC-Treaty is a first step towards an internationally coordinated migration policy. It is valid, however, for the EC-members only. For Turkey as a non-member a re-examination of the agreement on migration policy with the EC from 1964 might be not only in the interest of the Turkish government but also the EC-immigration countries. A migration agreement could create the precondition needed to reap the positive impacts of free labor movements promised by the normative theory of international economics.

References

Abdel-Fadil, M. (1985), **The Economic Impact of International Migration with Special Reference to Workers' Remittances in Countries of the Middle East**. IUSSP (International Union for the Scientific Study of Population), International Population Conference 1985 (Florence, June 5-12, 1985), Vol. 3, Liège: IUSSP, 13-29.

Berry, R.A. (1974), Impact of Factor Emigration on the Losing Region, in: **Economic Record**, 50, 405-422.

Berry, R.A. and R. Soligo, R. (1969), Some Welfare Aspects of International Migration, in: **Journal of Political Economy**, 77, 778-794.

Bhagwati, J.N. (1984), Incentives and Disincentives: International Migration, in: **Weltwirtschaftliches Archiv**, 120, 678-701.

Bhagwati, J.N. and T.N. Srinivasan (1983), On the Choice between Capital and Labor Mobility, in: **Journal of International Economics**, 14, 209-221.

Böhning, W.R. (1984), **Studies in International Labour Migration**. St. Martin's Press, New York.

Calvo, G. and S. Wellisz (1983), International Factor Mobility and National Advantage, in: **Journal of International Economics**, 14, 222-241.

Cases Mendez, J.I. and O. Cabezas Moro (1976), The Relation between Migration Policy and Economic Development and the

Promotion of New Employment Possibilities for Returnees, in: **International Migration**, 14, 134-162.

Choucri, N. and S. Lahiri (1983), **Macroeconomic Impacts of Remittances in Egypt: An Explanatory Analysis**. Technology Adaptation Program, MIT (TAP Report 83), Cambridge.

Galenson, W. and H. Leibenstein (1955), Investment Criteria, Productivity, and Economic Development, in: **Quarterly Journal of Economics**, 69, 343-370.

Galor, O. (1986), Time Preference and International Labor Migration, in: **Journal of Economic Theory**, 38, 1-20.

Gendt, van, R. (1977), **Return Migration and Reintegration Services**. OECD, Paris.

Gerking, S.D. and J.H. Mutti (1983), Factor Rewards and the International Migration of Unskilled Labor: A Model with Capital Mobility, in: **Journal of International Economics**, 14, 367-380.

Grossman, G.M. (1984), The Gains from International Factor Movements, in: **Journal of International Economics**, 17, 73-83.

Grubel, H. and A.D. Scott, (1966), The International Flow of Human Capital, in: **American Economic Review**, 56, 268-274.

Hamilton, C. and L.E.O. Svensson (1983), On the Choice between Capital Import and Labor Export, in: **European Economic Review**, 20, 167-192.

Hiemenz, U. und K.W. Schatz (1979), **Trade in Place of Migration**. ILO, Geneva.

Johnson, H.G. (1967), Some Economic Aspects of the Brain Drain, in: **Pakistani Development Review**, 7, 379-411.

Jones, R.W. et al. (1986), The Theory of International Factor Flows: The Basic Model, in: **Journal of International Economics**, 20, 313-327.

Kemp, M.C. (1964), **The Pure Theory of International Trade**. Prentice-Hall, Englewood Cliffs.

Kenen, P.B. (1971), Migration the Terms of Trade and Economic Welfare in the Source Country, in: Bhagwati J.N. et al. (eds.), **Trade, Balance of Payments and Growth**. Amsterdam, North-Holland, 238-260.

Kindleberger, C.P. (1965), Emigration and Economic Growth, in: **Banca Nazionale del Lavoro, Quarterly Review**, 18, 235-254.

Kuhn, P. and I. Wooton (1987), International Factor Movements in the Presence of a Fixed Factor, in: **Journal of International Economics**, 22, 123-140.

Lewis, A. (1954), Economic Development with Unlimited Supplies of Labour, in: **Manchester School of Economic and Social Studies**, 22, 139-191.

Lucas, R.E.B. (1981), International Migration: Economic Causes, Consequences and Evaluation, in: Kritz, M.M., et al. (eds.), **Global Trends in Migration**. Staten Island (N.Y.) Center for Migration Studies, 84-109.

Lundahl, M. (1985), International Migration, Remittances and Real Incomes: Effects on the Source Country, in: **Scandinavian Journal of Economics**, 87, 647-657.

Lutz, V. (1961), Some Structural Aspects of the Southern Problem: The Complementarity of 'Emigration' and Industrialization, in: **Banca Nazionale del Lavoro, Quarterly Review**, 14, 367-402.

MacDougall, G.D.A. (1960), The Benefits and Costs of Private Investment from Abroad: A Theoretical Approach, in: **Economic Record**, 36, 13-35.

Martin, P.L. and A. Richards (1980), International Migration of Labor: Boon or Bane? in: **Monthly Labor Review**, 103 (10), 4-9.

Myrdal, G. (1956), **An International Economy**. Harper & Row, New York.

OECD (1975), **The OECD and International Migration**. OECD, Paris.

OECD (1978), **The Migratory Chain**. OECD, Paris.

OECD (1979), **Migration, Growth and Development**. OECD, Paris.

OECD and SOPEMI (1973), **SOPEMI (Système d'Observation Permanente des Migrations)**, various Reports from 1973 to 1985. OECD, Paris.

Penninx, R. (1982), A Critical Review of Theory and Practice: The Case of Turkey, in: **International Migration Review**, 16, 781-818.

Paine, S. (1974), **Exporting Workers: The Turkish Case**. Cambridge University Press, Cambridge.

Ramaswami, V.K. (1968), International Factor Movement and the National Advantage, in: **Economica**, 35, 309-310.

Ranis, G. and J.C.H. Fei (1961), A Theory of Economic Development, in: **American Economic Review**, 51, 533-565.

Rivera-Batiz, F.L. (1982), International Migration, Non-Traded Goods and Economic Welfare in the Source Country, in: **Journal of Development Economics**, 2, 81-90.

——— (1984), International Migration, Non-Traded Goods and Economic Welfare in a Two-Class Economy, in: **Journal of Development Economics**, 16, 325-330.

Rogers, R. (1981), Incentives to Return: Patterns of Policies and Migrants' Responses, in: Kritz, M.M., et al. (eds.), **Global Trends in Migration**. Staten Island (N.Y.): Center for Migration Studies, 338-364.

Ruffin, R.J. (1981), Trade and Factor Movements with three Factors and two Goods, in: **Economic Letters**, 7, 177-182.

——— (1984), International Factor Movements, in: Jones, R.W. and P.B. Kenen (eds.), **Handbook of International Economics**, Vol. I. Amsterdam/New, York/Oxford, North-Holland, 237 -288.

Stahl, C.W. (1982), Labor Emigration and Economic Development, in: **International Migration Review**, 16, 869-899.

Straubhaar, T. (1983), **Arbeitskräftewanderung und Zahlungsbilanz**. Paul Haupt, Bern/Stuttgart.

——— (1985), The Balance of Payments Effect for their Home Country of Migrant Workers' Remittances, in: **Jahrbücher für Nationalökonomie und Statistik**, 200, 280-297.

——— (1988), **On the Economics of International Labor Migration**. Paul Haupt, Bern/Stuttgart.

Svensson, L.E.O. (1984), Factor Trade and Goods Trade, in: **Journal of International Economics**, 16, 365-378.

Swamy, G. (1985), Population and International Migration, in: **World Bank Staff Working Paper No. 689**. Washington: World Bank.

Thomas, B. (1958), **Economics of International Migration**. Macmillan, London.

——— (1973), **Migration and Economic Growth (A Study of Great Britain & the Atlantic Economy)**. (2nd edition) Cambridge University Press, London/New York.

Thompson, H. (1984), International Migration, Non-Traded Goods and Economic Welfare in the Source Country: A Comment, in: **Journal of Development Economics**, 16, 321-324.

Todaro, M.P. (1980), Internal Migration in Developing Countries: A Survey, in: Easterlin, R.A. (ed.), **Population and Economic Change in Developing Countries**. University of Chicago Press, Chicago, 361- 390.

——— (1985), **Economic Development in the Third World**. (3rd ed.) Longman, New York.

Weiner, M. (1985), On International Migration and International Relations, in: **Population and Development Review**, 11, 441-455.

Wong, K.-Y. (1983), On Choosing Among Trade in Goods and International Capital and Labor Mobility (A Theoretical Analysis), in: **Journal of International Economics**, 14, 223-250.

——— (1986), The Economic Analysis of International Migration: A Generalization, in: **Canadian Journal of Economics**, 19, 357-362.

IV. Migration Within Developing Countries

Rural – Urban Migration

On the Allocation of Risks in Developing Countries

Renate Schubert

Abstract: In developing countries, for several decades, massive net rural-urban migration has been observed. Such migration can be interpreted as resulting from attempts to realize an optimal allocation of individual risks. However, in fact, the allocation of individual and collective risks is sub-optimal. The identification of main reasons for the failure of rural-urban migration is indispensable for improving welfare in developing countries.

1. Introduction

In developing countries, for several decades, massive rural-urban migration has been observed. Although reverse migration, i.e. urban-rural migration, has also been observed (Day et al. (1987), 940), rural-urban migration streams are dominant.

There are several types of rural-urban migration: Migration with or without planned return, migration of single persons or of families, (contracted) migration with or (speculative) migration without future work contract (Bhattacharyya (1985), 56; Hunt/Kau (1985), 699; Stark (1985), 2; Molho (1986), 397). Yet, in this paper, differences between these types will not be considered. As typical case, a single migrant without planned return and without future work contract will be assumed.

Obviously, rural-urban migration very often proves to be unsatisfactory for individual migrants as well as for their families and for the developing countries themselves. In urban areas about 50% of the average annual population growth rate of 4 - 7% is due to rural-urban migration (Caldwell (1968), 5-11; Byerlee (1974), 543; Todaro (1976), 8-18; Lubell (1978), 747-748). Since the modern urban sector is expanding at a rate much lower than urban population, the number of persons searching for work in the formal sector is increasing. Furthermore, about 30% of the work force in the formal sector is underemployed (Todaro (1976), 16-17; Gillis et al. (1983), 180-184). As a consequence, the informal urban sector is growing at high rates, covering 30-70% of the whole urban work force (Sethuraman (1976), 70-71; Brown/Sanders (1981), 161-168). This constellation yields an expansion of slums and a reduction of average urban infrastructure services as well as a reduction of average urban wage and nutrition levels. On the other hand, in the rural areas average output typically decreases, at least if workers with high qualifications migrate (Berry/Soligo (1968); Marshall (1982), 165-166), implying that the economic and presumably also the political situation in rural areas deteriorates.

Nevertheless, neither individuals, their families nor developing nations seem to abstain from or to impede rural-urban migration. Furthermore, a seemingly paradoxial phenomenon can be stated (Stiglitz (1974), 194-195; Stiglitz (1976)): By means of migration, the rural population increases the urban unemployment and decreases rural output. Rural-urban wage differences are reduced but, as a matter of fact, do not vanish. Therefore, one can suppose that rural-urban migration is a special device which the agents considered here, esteem appropriate for achieving their aims. Thus, the motivating *questions* to be dealt with in the following are:

(A) What are the aims that agents pursue by realizing, promoting or tolerating rural-urban migration? In other words, why do agents not abstain from or impede such migration?

(B) For which reasons does rural-urban migration give unsatisfactory results? In other words, why are the aims pursued not reached?

(C) Which measures can be taken in order to render rural-urban migration less unsatisfactory? Or, under which conditions can rural-urban migration contribute to reaching the above mentioned aims?

Answering question (A) seems to be of fundamental importance and will be dealt with first. The hypothesis considered relevant for the answer will be explained in Section 3. The hypothesis itself implies a relationship between rural-urban migration and the perception and allocation of risks in developing countries. Therefore, in Section 2, such risks will be defined and described. In the remaining Sections 4 and 5, questions (B) and (C) will be discussed. Finally, in Section 6, some summarizing conclusions will be drawn.

2. Risks in Developing Countries

This section is divided into two parts: First, a general notion of risk as well as a short classification of risks will be given. Then, the special character of risks in developing countries will be considered.

In economics, the *notion of risk* is not unambiguous. With respect to the main topic of this paper, it seems unnecessary to report the broad discussion of the meaning of "risk". Nevertheless, three main notions of risk should be mentioned. Behind all three notions, there is a common basis: Risk exists if a decision-maker does not know with certainty the future outcome of alternatives he is to choose (Krelle (1968), 119 fn; Sinn (1986), 557).

Then, according to the first notion, risk may be interpreted as the existence of stochastic uncertainty (Knight (1921), 233; Borch (1969), 41; Röpke (1977), 128-130). This means a decision-maker is able to state a unique and precise probability distribution for all possible future states of the world, i.e., for all possible future outcomes of the alternatives considered.

According to the second notion, risk means the existence of the phenomenon that future outcomes of an alternative may be above or below a certain "normal" or expected outcome (Domar/Musgrave (1944); Tobin (1958); Sinn (1986), 557).

The third notion of risk, finally, is the existence of the phenomenon that future outcomes of an alternative may be below a "normal" or expected outcome. In other words: The existence of the possibility of future losses can be identified as risk (Krelle (1957), 632-633; Schneider (1980), 65).

One can show that this third notion of risk is of special relevance. Stochastic uncertainty can be transformed into a certainty constellation, using average outcomes as certain outcomes, at which point risk is no longer the decision-maker's problem. Furthermore, one can argue that for any decision-maker, potential losses represent a serious problem. Potential gains, on the other hand, often imply indirectly potential losses. If a decision-maker knew his future gains with certainty, he could dispose of them in advance. Being unable to do this by means of non-contingent contracts means being confronted with opportunity costs. So, in many cases, potential deviations of future outcomes from "normal" or expected outcomes can be characterized as *potential loss*. Therefore, the third notion of risk can be considered the most relevant one.

This view is supported by various empirical studies on the behavior of decision-makers under "risk" (MacCrimmon/Wehrung (1986)).

Throughout the rest of this paper, risk should be understood in the sense of the third notion mentioned above.

A general *classification of risks* can be made with respect to the variables concerned and with respect to the risks' extent or reasons. The *variables concerned* are monetary, material or non-monetary, non-material ones. They can be directly or indirectly affected by the danger of losses.

The *extent of a risk* depends on the extent of possible negative outcome deviations as well as on the level of subjective probability of future losses. Furthermore, the extent of risk depends on the importance a decision-maker attaches to possible future losses given by a certain extent of loss and degree of belief in that loss.

The aforementioned typology refers to individuals as well as to collective risks. In general, *individual risks* are defined as risks which accrue to a single decision-maker or, to a small group of decision-makers respectively, who are able to shift at least parts of their risk to other persons or institutions. *Collective or social risks* on the other hand, accrue simultaneously to a great number of economic agents, who, as a rule, are unable to shift their risks on to other agents.

Finally, with respect to *reasons for risks*, one can differentiate between exogenous and endogenous reasons. Exogenous reasons prevail if the considered decision-maker is not responsible for the existence of the risk. If reasons are endogenous, they are produced by the decision-maker himself, for instance due to lack of information or control.

Considering developing countries, various types of risks, in the sense of possible futures losses, can be stated. In the following, risks which are connected with the rural-urban migration phenomenon predominate. First, there are individual risks which accrue to the potential migrants as well as to their families (concerning the importance of families see Caldwell (1968), 56-86; Mincer (1978), 757-760; Chang (1981), 316-325; Da Vanzo (1981); Harbison (1981); Hugo (1981); Caces et al. (1985)).

The *potential migrants' risks* can be described as follows: If potential migrants stay in the rural area, they face a possible future loss of income and standard of living compared with income and standard of living they could realize if their urban status were successful. Their urban status would be successful if they could work in the formal or modern urban sector and if they could achieve at least the average amount of material and non-material urban infrastructure. If they migrate to the urban area, they face a possible future loss of income and standard of living compared with the income and standard of living they could realize in the rural area. Such a loss occurs if the migrants' urban status is not successful, i.e. if they were without work or had a low-paying work and if they were participating less than average in the urban infrastructure. Furthermore, they might not receive any support from their former rural network. Besides, there is also an immaterial risk as far as the existence of social network is concerned. Migrants face the risk of leaving their familiar rural network and all the support it may give, without being incorporated into a new urban network.

The *families' risks* consist of the following: If the potential migrants stay, they face the potential future loss of their cost of living being increasingly higher than the output they produce. If the potential migrants leave the rural area, the families face the risk of having a lower rural output and therefore, a lower standard of living if the migrants' output cannot be sufficiently substituted. Furthermore, families are confronted with the non-material risk of weakening the rural social network when the potential migrants drop out.

In addition, *risks of the urban entrepreneurs* can be identified. The risk they face when rural-urban migration takes place is the danger of a decrease in the quality of the work done in their firms or, respectively, a decrease in productivity, i.e., an increase in cost per labor unit if they employ the enormously increasing urban work force. Such losses could arise due to an increase in shirking, in labor turnover, by an increase in the number of worker subject to the adverse selection phenomenon or by a decrease in gift exchange between the entrepreneur and his workers (Leibenstein (1963),

62-93; Stiglitz (1974), 197-227; Stiglitz (1976); Akerlof (1984); Yellen (1984); Schlicht (1987)). If rural-urban migration does not take place, urban entrepreneurs face the risk of being confronted with a work force too small to produce the amounts of factors or commodities they would be able to sell.

Rural entrepreneurs, on the other hand, face the same risk of having too small a work force in the case of rural-urban migration. Furthermore, they face the risk of losing their best workers due to migration to the urban areas. In case of no migration, however, they are confronted with risks similar to those of urban entrepreneurs in the migration case. This means, the less migration there is, the higher might be the risk of low quality, low productivity and high cost per labor unit in rural production.

Now let us consider *collective or social risks* connected with rural-urban migration. They accrue to a developing country as a whole. These collective potential future losses consist of a decrease in productivity, in national output and in standard of living. Furthermore, nationwide unemployment may increase, urban fertility may increase, education level and average material and non-material infrastructure may decrease (Berry/Soligo (1968), 231; Usher (1977), 1001; Gillis et al. (1983), 180-189; Simon/Heins (1985), 86-89).

Such losses may occur if net rural-urban migration takes place, caused by the aforementioned *overpopulation* of the urban areas, or on the other hand, if there is *no* rural-urban migration. Then, an under-utilization of urban production and infrastructure capacities might be the reason for a very low rate of technical progress throughout the whole country.

Finally, connected with these collective risks, there are risks accruing to *governmental institutions*. Such institutions, especially their individual members, face the risk of losing reputation, power and even their priviledged positions if the whole country suffers from the aforementioned losses.

Being informed about the risks in developing countries related to rural-urban migration, one can now proceed to analyze the reasons why agents do not abstain from or impede such migration. As the next section will show, perception and allocation of the risks described in this section will play a crucial role.

3. Reasons for the Persistence of Rural-Urban Migration

In most economic migration models, the main reason for rural-urban migration, assuming similar cost of living in rural and urban areas, is that the expected urban income or, respectively, the stream of discounted future urban income exceeds the expected rural income or the stream of discounted future rural income. Sometimes this reason is presented in a different way, such that rural-urban migration occurs only if expected income in the urban subsistence sector is higher than in the rural subsistence sector and if there is a positive probability for changing from urban subsistence sector to urban modern sector (Todaro (1969), 141-146; Harris/Todaro (1970); Johnson (1971); Godfrey (1973); Fields (1975); Todaro (1976), 30-53; Bhatia (1979); Gillis et al. (1983), 190-209; Bhattacharyya (1985); Cole/Sanders (1985); Schubert (1985); Molho (1986); Berninghaus/Seifert-Vogt (1987); Straubhaar (1987)).

However, such explanations seem *unsatisfactory* because of two reasons: First, only monetary or at least material determinants seem to be relevant for making a migration decision. Yet, for individual decision-makers, non-material determinants should also be considered. Second, the agents' information and perception structure assumed in these models does not seem very plausible. At least, findings concerning information and perception structure of decision-makers, influencing the decision-making process and its results, are hardly taken into account. Therefore, the central hypothesis of this paper is that rural-urban migration is viewed as device to bring about an optimal allocation of the individual and therefore also the collective risks described above. As long as private and governmental agents cling to rural-urban migration as instrument in striving for an optimal risk allocation, this type of migration will persist.

The question to be dealt with now concerns the reasons for which rural-urban migration can be viewed as *device for an optimal risk allocation*. Furthermore, one has to answer the question why agents are interested in an optimal risk allocation. The answers to both questions require a discussion of some principles of risk perception and measurement, which will be analyzed next.

3.1. Risk Perception and Measurement

In order to compare different alternatives, e.g. migration and non-migration, their differences in risk may be considered, requiring a cardinal measurement, referring to the same variable. On such a basis, risks concerning different or numerous variables can be amalgamated according to the decision-maker's preference list.

Risk measurement has been discussed in economic literature for the case of unique and precise, i.e. *quantitative probability information*. In this case, statistical characteristics like standard deviation, semi-variance, higher moments of probability distributions, etc., are suggested as risk measures (Schneeweiß (1967), 52-57; Krelle (1968), 148-159; Sinn (1980), 57-58). Furthermore, a decision-maker's attitude toward risk is typically expressed by his risk-preference function or by his dispersion-preference function (Krelle (1968), 138-159. On the basis of such a function, absolute or relative risk aversion, risk neutrality or risk proneness can be defined (Pratt (1964); Arrow (1970)).

In this paper, using such measurement concepts is problematic because of two reasons. First, most concepts do not match the notion of risk given here. Second, and more important, the assumed decision-maker's state of information does not seem relevant, at least in the migration context. Potential migrants, their families, rural and urban employers, and governmental institutions will not have unique and precise probability distributions on future states of world, i.e. on future outcomes of alternatives. Normally, they would not have the capacity or willingness required to construct such probability distributions.

However, their state of information may be characterized as *partial probability information*. This means they are able to compare every two elements out of the set of various future states of world which they think relevant and possible. They can indicate whether the first state is more probable, less probable or equally probable than the second state. In this way, they may be able to rank the outcomes thought relevant and possible with respect to probability.

Yet, this ranking will only be ordinal or qualitative. Precise differences in probability between different states of world will generally not be known.

If qualitative or partial probability rankings are accepted as relevant for the agents considered, the question is how such rankings are constructed. Usually, agents are not equiped with such rankings but have to build them up themselves. For the process of constructing such rankings, *perception of risk* is of crucial importance.

A large amount of literature exists concerning human perception (cf. for instance various authors from "Gestalttheorie" such as Metzger (1931); Wertheimer (1945); Köhler (1947); Asch (1952); Heider (1960)). There is much less literature concerning especially risk perception (cf. for instance Kuhnreuter et al. (1985); Rapoport (1987)). However, the general principles of perception seem appropriate to be conferred also to the phenomenon of risk perception. Some of these principles can be interpreted as being of special importance; they will be reported in the following (cf. for instance Allais (1953), 503; Kahneman/Tversky (1979); Tversky/Kahneman (1981); Kahneman et al. (1982); Kahneman/Tversky (1982), 154-157; Rapoport (1987)).

The question of which risks, and to what extent they are perceived, depends on the framing of the situations in which risks are to be perceived. Such framing includes the character of alternatives to choose. It also includes the outcome characterization (for instance, gains or losses) and the social network (i.e. all types of conventions, prejudices and morales) with which a decision-maker is confronted.

Beside the framing, aspects of *prägnanz* or simplicity determine (risk) perception. When perceiving future outcomes of alternatives, a decision-maker concentrates on very few characteristics. Those characteristics selected depend on the personal characteristics of the decision-maker, the availability of experience with similar characteristics, the peculiarity of characteristics, etc. Normally, one of the few characteristics dominates the others, as in a lexicographic ordering.

Finally, some inertia in perception is important. A phenomenon, for instance a risk, perceived in a certain way, will typically be perceived in the same way throughout a certain period of time, regardless of whether its "objective" appearance changed or not. Only if radical changes take place, perception typically adapts.

With special regard to risk perception, the following effects are relevant. First, the simpler a decision situation is perceived, i.e. different alternatives and their outcomes, the less probable are perceived negative outcome deviations. Second, very small probabilities are usually identified with zero probabilities. Furthermore, small probabilities are perceived higher and high probabilities are perceived lower than their objective counterparts. There is a general tendency to observe that decision-makers perceive alternatives with high possible future losses and relatively low probabilities as less risky than alternatives with relatively low possible future losses and high probabilities, even if the mathematical expectation of both alternatives is identical (Kunreuther et al. (1985)). Presumably, this observable tendency is due to the above described general perception principle of *prägnanz*. On average, decision-makers experience small losses more often than large losses. Therefore, they are more prone to consider them as relevant future outcome of their alternatives. Having reported some perception characteristics which might be important for the construction of qualitative probability rankings, one can now proceed to consider the *measurement of risk* and risk sensitivity in the case of *qualitative probability information*.

Risk measures are thought of as a numerical representation of a given risk structure, assigning a numerical risk value to each alternative considered. The development of such a risk measure requires the development of a system of axioms characterizing the decision-maker's risk perception. In this paper, reporting such system of axioms would be too far removed from the main topic. So it might be sufficient here to refer to work which already has been done in this field (Brachinger (1989)).

One can develop a system of axioms which is consistent with the risk perception principles mentioned above. Furthermore, one can show that there exists a numerical representation of this risk structure. A function, representing such risk measure, will contain certain parameters characterizing the decision-maker's risk-sensitivity. Further, individual risks may be summed to indicate collective risks. Such a summation seems to be a plausible concept since a transfer of individual risks to the collective, such that the collective risk is lower than the sum of all individual risks, is not possible. It may be possible, that some members of the group considered bear risks of others without perceiving them as risks. However, this has something to do with the allocation, not with the measurement of risk. Therefore, this cannot be a relevant argument in the present context.

Having discussed the questions of perception and measurement of risk, one can now return to the question of how the decision-makers, considered in the migration context, cope with the risks they are confronted with. How do they proceed, when deciding whether to migrate or not, whether to tolerate or support rural-urban migration or not? Which alternative do the agents choose and why? These are the questions to answer in the following section.

3.2 Attractiveness of Rural-Urban Migration

Let us, first, consider the potential migrants' decision. Potential migrants are confronted with the decision problem of staying in rural areas or migration to urban areas. The material and non-material future outcomes of each alternative are uncertain. They depend, of course, on individual characteristics of the potential migrants, e.g. their rural employment and income, their race, age, sex, education, skills, professional experiences, etc. (Lee (1966), 50-52); Mac Donald/Mac Donald (1969); Shaw (1975), 13-15; De Jong/Fawcett (1981), 26-30). Often, as mentioned before, in migration literature only the material or monetary outcome components are stressed (Harris/Todaro (1970); Johnson (1971); Speare (1971); Bhatia (1979); Lucas (1985)). However, such a perspective seems too narrow. Therefore, in the following, outcomes will always include both components, material and non-material ones.

Having to decide between various alternatives, a *decision-maker's calculus, based on the existence of partial probability information*, can be described as follows: Choosing an alternative, the decision-maker wants to realize a certain minimum aspiration level concerning the outcome, represented, for instance, by means of an outcome vector. Therefore, he may first divide all relevant alternatives into two groups: One group will consist of alternatives held appropriate to yield the aspiration level. The other group will consist of the rest of alternatives, held inappropriate to yield the desired aspiration level.

In order to differentiate between these two groups despite the uncertainty of future outcomes, the decision-maker might use the device of considering *quasi-certain states of world.* A state of world may be named quasi-certain if it is the state of world which the decision-maker thinks by far most probable to prevail . In other words, regardless of the special alternative considered, it is the state of world, which always is number one in the decision-maker's probability ranking. So, a decision-maker will choose an alternative out of the group of alternatives which, for the quasi-certain state of world, will fulfill his outcome requirements. These alternatives will be named *admissible alternatives*.

Solving this choice problem, the decision-maker's criterion might be the minimizing of risks. This means a decision-maker will be prone to choose an alternative which, on one hand, is admissible in the sense of yielding a minimum outcome aspiration level in the quasi-certain case, and which, on the other hand, involves the lowest risk possible. Such a *decision procedure*, yielding alternatives which, in the quasi-certain case, deliver a near-optimal result and which, in the case of deviations from the quasi-certain case, deliver "relatively good" results, i.e. low risk results, may be called *robust* (Brachinger (1982), 11-132).

The choice of an alternative which gives way to risk minimizing subject to some minimum outcome requirements can be identified as guaranteeing an optimal risk allocation. What is to be understood by "*optimal risk allocation*"?

First, the phenomenon of the allocation of risks can be discussed in the following way: Risk, in the sense of the possibility of future losses, may be seen neither as a commodity nor as a factor of production, but as an involuntary tribute to pay whenever a decision (with uncertain consequences) is to be made (Schubert (1988a)). Then, the allocation aspect has two components: first, the determination of the total height of risk for a society and, second, the risk incidence with respect to the different members of a society.

As far as total height of risk is concerned, one can say that a risk allocation is optimal if the involuntary tributes which have to be paid are minimized. In other words, a risk allocation is optimal if the extent of individual and collective risks does not exceed the inevitable amount of risks, which is determined by the outcome aspiration levels which prevail. In general, one can say that the higher these aspiration levels are, the higher will be the inevitable risks. However, independent of the size of these inevitable risks, avoiding excess burden in the sense of minimizing risks given certain outcome aspiration levels can be characterized as optimal. Therefore, the decision behavior described above can be seen as necessary condition for realizing an optimal risk allocation. Obviously, at this point, individual decision making goals and collective goals coincide.

As far as *risk incidence* is concerned, the distribution of inevitable risks on individual agents or groups of agents is alluded to. In general, every agent is able to shift at least part of his risks on to other agents. Every transfer of risk, whether done by explicit or implicit contracts, will have its price. With regard to this incidence aspect, risk allocation can be called globally optimal if each agent belonging to the group or nation considered is bearing the amount of risks which corresponds to his willingness to bear risks. In other words, with regard to the incidence aspect, any risk allocation is optimal which in case of a slight change in allocation, would deteriorate the welfare of at least one agent, the welfare of the others being constant. In this context, the willingness to bear risks depends as well on the ability as on the proneness of individual agents to bear such risks.

Of course, the aforementioned arguments hold only for individual risks. The incidence of collective risks which are characterized by the fact that they cannot be shifted except to members of other groups or nations will always be such that at least one agent belonging to the group or nation considered will have to bear more risks than he is willing to bear. Therefore, a globally optimal allocation with respect to the incidence aspect may not exist. If it does not exist, it seems plausible to assume that the required outcome aspiration levels no longer imply a general consensus throughout the group or nation considered.

A single decision-maker confronted with the incidence problem, i.e. with the problem of risk bearing, will take this aspect into consideration already when choosing his alternative. This means he will minimize an admissible alternative's risk which he has to bear, subject to *risk bearing contracts* he makes with other agents before actual losses occur. However, the existence of such risk-shifting contracts brings about new risks, namely those of breaching of contracts. So, when deciding on an alternative, a decision-maker will also take into consideration these risks in the way described before. Choosing an admissible alternative with minimal risk also means, then, that the decision-makers's contracting risks are minimal, subject to a required quasi-certain minimum risk-shifting. Such minimization induces, of course, a certain type of risk-shifting contract. However, a general discussion of this type cannot be given in this paper (see Schubert (1988a)).

Yet, the discussion of the incidence aspects alludes already to a further aspect of an optimal risk allocation. This further aspect is the *stability of alternatives* and contracts chosen. Such stability refers to the phenomenon of changes in risk components or risk perception between the moment of decision and the further outcome realization or shortly after outcome realization. It is in a decision-maker's interest, as well as in the interest of the group or nation considered, to make choices which are stable or robust with respect to the aforementioned changes. Otherwise, individual or collective welfare losses connected with permanent changes of actions and contracts would be considerably high. Guaranteeing a certain degree of stability is possible by using the robust decision procedure described above (Schubert (1988a)).

In the light of risk perception, risk measurement and decision making, let us now look at *a potential migrant's decision*. Typically he will choose the migration alternative for instance if, for the quasi-certain state of world, only rural-urban migration fulfills material and immaterial minimum outcome requirements. More plausibly, he will choose migration if, for deviations from the quasi-certain state of world, perceived risks of migration are smaller than those of non-migration, both alternatives being admissible with respect to quasi-certain minimum aspiration levels. Because of two reasons, it might be plausible, that perceived risks of rural-urban migration might appear smaller than those of non migration.

The first reason belongs to the *perception field*. Potential migrants usually do not have much "objective" and reliable information on their presumable chances in urban areas. To a high degree, they obtain their information from their rural friends who chose the migration alternative some time before them, and who, as a rule, present their migration decision as a success, regardless of their actual situation in the urban areas. Some material attributes, acquired in the urban area, may underline this impression. On the other hand, there are only some of these friends who, due to a failure in the urban area, dare to return to the rural areas. Therefore, the average perception that potential migrants may have when migrating is that there is a high probability that small losses may occur and a very low probability that high losses may occur, forcing migrants, for instance, to return back to their homes. According to the above described (risk) perception principles, this state of information may induce an underestimating of migration risk or an overestimating of non-migration risk respectively. Besides, given the scarce information on actual migration consequences, potential migrants may recognize migration as a simply structured alternative. Therefore, according to the perception principles described above, migration might be perceived as an almost riskless alternative. Furthermore, the effect of decision framing proposed by former migrants or agents trying to induce migration, should not be ignored. Then, rural-urban migration appears attractive.

The second reason for the migration alternative to appear relatively riskless stems from the *risk incidence phenomenon*. In developing countries, strong relations between individuals, i.e. potential migrants and their families or social network, can be observed. These relations can be interpreted as risk distribution constracts, releasing potential migrants from parts of theirs risks. Such contracts may be as follows: In case of migration, the potential migrant may be not successful. Then, he will be supported by his family. The price he pays for this support may consist of redemptions in the sense of transfers from the urban to the rural area if, in case of migration, the potential migrant will be successful. Such contracts can be advantageous not only to a potential migrant but also to his family. There may be a shift of migration risks as well as of risks the families have to bear independently of whether migration takes place or not, such as income risks due to unfavorable wheather conditions, diseases, etc. Due to the existence of the aforementioned redemptions, risks are not only shifted but also reduced.

Such private migrant-family contracts lessening individual migration risks are of predominant importance. Professional insurers cannot compete because private insurance premiums can be much lower than professional ones. This is due to the fact that, on one hand, a family has no financing cost in the case of successful migration and, on the other hand, a family can fulfill its duties form current surplus without backing it up with savings.

Finally, taking into consideration such migrant-family contracts, rural-urban migration may appear as an optimal alternative also with respect to the *stability criterion*. If a private insurance contract exists and is not breached, then rural-urban migration may be considered as diversification and therefore lessening of risks regarding the migrant-family network (for the case of diversification of income risks see Stark/Levhari (1982), 192-196). Including the possibility of mutual support will make a migration decision relatively stable, since independent of a certain range of changes in risk components or risk perceptions the losses to bear by the individuals or their families will not exceed the corresponding willingness and ability to bear these risks.

Obviously, in the real world, potential migrants choose a risk-minimizing alternative, subject to some outcome aspiration levels, taking into consideration incidence and stability aspects. Therefore, their decisions can be described as attempts to realize an optimal risk allocation.

Let us now consider the attractiveness of rural-urban migration for other agents beside the potential migrants. As far as the *migrants' families* are concerned, it was already mentioned that in combination with migrant-family contracts, families may consider rural-urban migration as device for an optimal allocation of their migration risks. Therefore, they have no reason to hinder potential migrants from choosing the migration alternative.

Next, *urban entrepreneurs* will be considered. The question is: Why do they not impede rural-urban migration by lowering urban wage levels to such extent that rural-urban wage differences disappear. According to market principles usually propagated, such wage decrease should be the consequence of the immense increase of urban labor supply due to rural-urban migration. However, keeping urban wages at a relatively high level, i.e. at a level higher than the market clearing level, can be interpreted as the entrepreneurs' attempt to realize an optimal risk allocation. With reference to the entrepreneurial risks mentioned in section 2., one can conclude that non-migration risks are relatively irrelevant looking at the actual economic situation in developing countries. On the contrary, migration risks dominate. However, having migration together with setting wages at a relatively high level according to the efficiency wage hypothesis (Akerlof (1984); Yellen (1984)) can be interpreted as the result of a robust decision procedure. Such choice guarantees a given entrepreneurial outcome aspiration level, not endangered by the case of non-migration. At the same time, due to the productivity stimulating effect of high wages, it probably produces only small negative deviations from the desired outcome. Therefore, tolerating or even motivating rural-urban migration by keeping average urban wages high can be described as optimizing risk allocation from the urban entrepreneurs' point of view.

As far as *rural entrepreneurs* are concerned, having migration together with a low average rural wage and some high wages for a few highly qualified workers may also be considered as the result of a robust decision procedure. Such choice guarantees a given entrepreneurial outcome aspiration level being above the average level attainable in the non-migration case. At the same time, due to the agricultural wage structure, it probably produces relatively small possible future outcome losses. Therefore, tolerating or even motivating rural-urban migration by keeping average rural wage low can be described as optimizing risk allocation form the rural entrepreneurs' point of view.

Finally, *governmental institutions* have to be analyzed concerning their attitude on rural-urban migration. In developing countries, it is generally observable that governments strive for and believe in reputation by creating enormous production and infrastructure capacities in urban areas, mainly in capitals. Then, non-migration risks seem to become predominant as compared to migration risks, so that not impeding rural-urban migration appears as the optimal alternative with respect to the risks involved. This tendency might be strengthened by some risk perception effects. For many members of governmental institutions, personal reputation matters much more directly than (decreasing) national product or average standard of living do. Furthermore, the gap between the developing countries' population and the governmental institutions' leaders is considerable, so that for these leaders the urban overpopulation effects are hardly noticeable. Therefore, these leaders' perception of rural-urban migration risks will be such that these risks are relatively small and therefore negligible. So, even for governmental institutions, rural-urban migration can be interpreted as an alternative useful for striving at an optimal risk allocation.

However, observation in developing countries shows, that actual consequences of rural-urban migration are such that, obviously, *risks are not optimally allocated*. Neither of the groups considered seems to realize its desired outcome level and to bear the amount of risk it is able and prone to bear. Therefore, in the next section, one has to analyze why the attempts to realize an optimal risk allocation fail.

4. Reasons for the Failure of the Rural-Urban Migration

Obviously, rural-urban migration results as failure for most of the migrants as well as for their families and for developing countries in their entirety. Nevertheless, as described in the previous section, agents seem to have no motivation to abstain from or to impede such migration. Therefore, the question is: Why does rural-urban migration result in failure, although it appears attractive to all groups of concerned agents. In other words, why do individual and collective rationality diverge?

In part, the reasons lie in the selection process different agents, in particular potential migrants, use to select their optimal alternative, i.e. migration. There are two critical points as far as this selection process is concerned:

First, as mentioned above, (risk) *perception* plays a dominant role for the level of risk attached to different alternatives. Therefore, perception is decisive for the final choice, assuming that agents try to minimize their risks subject to certain outcome aspiration level conditions using a robust decision procedure. It was mentioned above, that there can be no objective risk perception. However, risk perception by potential migrants and governmental institutions hardly takes into consideration "objective" information obtainable by impartial observers. Such information concerns the actual situtation of former rural fellows who already migrated to urban areas. It equally concerns the actual situation of average urban or rural population. This lack of information means that risk perception is not adjusted to perceivable facts. This will inevitably lead to decisions not accounting for the facts. Therefore, as will be explained in the next section, one step to transform rural-urban migration form failure to success should be to exercise some influence on agents' risk perception.

Second, the existence of the *incidence contracts* described above is important for the migration alternative to appear attractive. However, the problem is whether such contracts are reliable or whether they are to be breached. Obviously, there is a cooperation problem. This cooperation problem has the form of a prisoners' dilemma problem. If both sides of the contract fulfill their duties, the contract is advantageous to both parties. However, if one party — for instance the potential migrant — does not fulfill its duties, the other party — for instance his familiy — is better off when equally not fulfilling its duties.

Such breaching of contract may be avoided if there are credible and relevant monetary or non-monetary sanctions to be applied to those who breach the contract. However, as far as the aforementioned migration contracts are concerned, such sanctions are scarcely observable. This means, voluntary cooperation must become effective. It may be presumed, that such voluntary cooperation often prevails in the context referred to here. It may be the consequence of some cooperation norm which has been developed and stabilized throughout a certain period of time. In its beginning, this norm might have been the rational result of some robust, conditionally risk minimizing decision process (Schubert (1987), 209-212).

However, there is no guarantee for cooperation to hold, i.e. for the described contracts not to be breached. Yet, if they are breached, then the migration alternative, implying such contract, must no longer be the optimal alternative. Therefore, as will be explained in the next section, another step to transform rural-urban migration from failure to success should be to make voluntary cooperation more reliable.

In addition to the selection process, the *role of wages and rural-urban wage differentials* is important for the persistence of rural-urban migration. As described in the previous section, according to the entrepreneurs' attempt to realize optimal risk allocation, wages or wage differentials fulfill certain functions within the firms. They do not balance labor supply and demand. Due to this phenomenon, no rural-urban population balancing takes place. Therefore, in order to produce such balancing, further precaution might be appropriate to render rural-urban migration a success. Such precaution should be either to find a variable different from wage to control productivity within firms. Alternatively, one should find a variable different from wage to balance labor markets and rural-urban population distribution.

In the next section, the above mentioned three types of measures for successful rural-urban migration will be explained in detail.

5. Measures to Render Rural-Urban Migration a Success

The first measure is to base agents' risk perception on more realistic information concerning actual migration consequences. Second, the existence of voluntary cooperation, i.e. the avoidance of contract breaching, should be strengthened. Third, intra-firm productivity goals and labor market clearing should be separated instrumentally. In the following, some more detailed measures are proposed to make these different types of measures effective.

With respect to influencing risk perception, a *change in information policy* seems adequate. This means that governmental institutions should provide more information about actual consequences of rural-urban migration, such as housing, work, infrastructure facilities, etc. They should describe as many aspects of the urban overpopulation, labor demand deficiency problems and rural de-population problems as possible. Such information, of course, should be provided free of charge for its users.

Conversely , on the other hand, economic agents, especially potential migrants and their families, should be provided with information recognition and processing capacities. Otherwise, the information intensification activities mentioned above would be useless. Improving information recognition and processing capacities means that decision-makers will be able to take into consideration a larger range of oberservations of reality than before when constructing future states of world. Therefore, they will consider a larger range of possible future outcomes of alternatives which they think to be relevant.

Moreover, economic agents might become able to take into consideration a longer period of time than before. Typically, in developing countries, decision-makers are rather myopic, considering no or only few future periods of time. With respect to a more realistic risk perception, an enlargement of decision-making horizon seems to be useful.

Furthermore, application of decision-making techniques, such as the robust decision procedure, which until now have been applied more or less intuitively, should be made more conscious and should be trained. Only then, decision-makers will be able to consider the officially provided information in an adequate way. With respect to this aim, intense decision-making training should also include recognition and simultaneous consideration of different aims. It should include as well the balancing of material or monetary and immaterial or non-monetary aims.

Experience in various developing countries shows that such information recognition and processing training can be realized quite successfully (Schubert (1988b)). However, in order to be successful, it will take a lot of time, money and intense care to invest. Yet, with respect to the success already realized and the serious nature of the problems to be solved, such investment seems worthwhile.

Finally, influencing risk perception could be exercized not only by information provision and decision-making training but also by definite actions. Such actions, transforming rural-urban migration from failure to success, could be a shift in the creation of new production, administration and infrastructure facilities from urban to rural areas, allowing a nation-wide diversification of attractive centers to be achieved, changing risk perception in such a way that none of these various centers would be confronted with the heavy overpopulation problems actually known.

Let us now consider the *stimulation of voluntary cooperation*. Obviously, the cooperation problem is the lack of confidence in the other agents' words or actions. An increase in confidence, of course, cannot be ordered. However, a basis can be created, favorable for growing confidence.

Creating such basis could, on one hand, be incorporated in the decision-making training mentioned before. Such training can serve the purpose of increasing the agents' consciousness for the advantages and for the importance of cooperation.

On the other hand, the creation of institutions backing contract parties which had been betrayed could be useful. Such institutions can be interpreted as "positive sanctions", in which they refund parties in monetary or non-monetary terms, e.g. in reputation terms, if they are victims of breach of contract. Knowledge of such background support will make it much easier and more attractive for economic agents to "risk" cooperation. This, of course, yields cooperation. Therefore, the creation of some sort of official reimbursement of funds, being more than refunded by the contract breachers in order to avoid funds' misuse, would be useful. Furthermore, some reward mechanisms for cooperators, such as official praise, should be introduced.

Finally, let us consider the third type of measure, i.e. the *instrumental separation of labor-market balance and intra-firm productivity goals*. According to studies concerning efficiency wage theory, wage seems to be an adequate variable controlling intra-firm productivity. Therefore, another variable controlling labor markets and, here implied, net migration streams should be found. This variable, in order to fulfill its function, must play an important role in the decision-makers' calculus. Such a variable could be a per-capita tax to be paid by migrants, supplemented by a per-capita subsidy for those remaining in rural areas (Schubert (1987), 219-220).

If other instruments could be found to control intra-firm productivity, then rural-urban wage differentials could serve as instrument to control net migration streams. This means instruments like organizational or reward incentive structures or market interlinkages (Mitra (1982)) should be propagated in order to render rural-urban migration a success.

6. Conclusions

As a rule, in developing countries, net rural-urban migration exists. Reasons can be identified for which migration appears attractive to the agents involved. Apart from the reasons identified in traditional migration models, one can identify other reasons lying in the agents' information structure and (risk) perception. Then, attempts to realize an optimal allocation of risks may be found as the main reason for rural-urban migration's attractive appearance.

However, actual migration results cannot be characterized as success concerning the optimality of risk allocation. This is mainly due to risk perception which excludes information on actual migration consequences. Furthermore, cooperation problems prevail.

Finally, migration balancing is difficult since the variable usually meant to manage this balance via balancing labor demand and supply has to fulfill a different function, i.e. to control intra-firm productivity.

Therefore, transforming rural-urban migration from failure to success implies influencing risk perception and decision-making, stimulating cooperation, and finding two instruments controlling the two goals of high intra-firm productivity and balanced labor demand and supply. Measures to make these steps are available, yet they will require a considerable amount of both time and money. However, with respect to the problems involved, i.e. the welfare of nations, such investment seems worthwhile.

References

Akerlof, G.A. (1984), Gift Exchange and Efficiency-Wage Theory: Four Views, in: **American Economic Review, Papers and Proceedings**, 74, 79-83.

Allais, M. (1953), Le comportement de l'homme rationnel devant le risque: Critiques des postulats et axiomes de l'ècole amèricaine, in: **Econometrica**, 21, 503-546.

Arrow, K.J. (1970), The Theory of Risk Aversion, in: K.J. Arrow (ed.), **Essays in the Theory of Risk-Bearing**, Amsterdam-London, 30-120.

Asch, S.E. (1952), **Social Psychology**, Englewood Cliffs.

Berninghaus, S. and H.G. Seifert-Vogt (1987), International Migration under Incomplete Information, in: **Schweizerische Zeitschrift für Volkswirtschaft und Statistik**, 123, 199-218.

Berry, R.A. and R. Soligo (1968), Rural-Urban Migration, Agricultural Output, and the Supply Price of Labour in a Labour-Surplus Economy, in: **Oxford Economic Papers**, 20, 230-249.

Bhatia, K.B. (1979), Rural-Urban Migration and Surplus Labour, in: **Oxford Economic Papers**, 31, 403-414.

Bhattacharyya, B. (1979), The role of Family Decision in Internal Migration — The Case of India, in: **Journal of Development Economics**, 18, 51-66.

Borch, K.H. (1969), **Wirtschaftliches Verhalten bei Unsicherheit**, Wien-München.

Brachinger, H.W. (1982), **Robuste Entscheidungen**, Heidelberg.

——— (1989), **Entscheidungen bei Risiko**, Tübingen, unpublished habilitation thesis.

Brown, L.A. and R.L. Sanders (1981), Toward a Development Paradigm of Migration, with Particular Reference to Third World Settings, in: G.F. De Jong, and R.W. Gardner (eds.), **Migration Decision Making**, New York, etc., 149- 185.

Byerlee, D. (1974), Rural-Urban Migration in Africa: Theory, Policy and Research Implications, in: **International Migration Review**, 30, 543-566.

Caces, F.A., J.T. Fawcett and R.W. Gardner (1985), Shadow Households and Competing Auspices, in: **Journal of Development Economics**, 17, 5-25.

Caldwell, J.C. (1968), **African Rural-Urban Migration, The Movement to Ghana's Towns**, Canberra-London.

Chang, T.H.P. (1981), A Review of Micro Migration Research in the Third World Context, in: G.F. De Jong and R.W. Gardner (eds.), **Migration Decision Making**, New York, etc., 303-327.

Cole, W.E. and R.D. Sanders (1985), Internal Migration and Urban Employment in the Third World, in: **American Economic Review**, 75, 481-494.

Da Vanzo, J. (1981), Microeconomic Approaches to Studying Migration Decisions, in: G.F. De Jong and R.W. Gardner (eds.), **Migration Decision Making**, New York, etc., 90-129.

Day, R., S. Dagupta, S.K. Datta and J.B. Nugent (1978), Instability in Rural-Urban Migration, in: **Economic Journal**, 97, 940-950.

De Jong. G.F. and J.T. Fawcett (1981), Motivations for Migration: An Assessment and a Value-Expectancy Research Model, in: G.F. De Jong and R.W. Gardner (eds.), **Migration Decision Making**, New York, etc., 13-58.

Domar, E.D. and R.A. Musgrave (1944), Proportional Income Taxation and Risk-Taking, in: **Quarterly Journal of Economics**, 58, 388-422.

Fields, G.S. (1975), Rural-Urban Migration, Urban Unemployment and Underemployment, and Job-Search Activity in LDC's, in: **Journal of Development Economics**, 2, 165-187.

Gillis, M., D.H. Perkins, M. Roemer and D.R. Snodgrass (1983), **Economics of Development**, New York-London, Chapter 8: Labor and Growth, 177-209.

Godfrey, E.M. (1973), Economic Variables and Rural-Urban Migration: Some Thoughts on the Todaro Hypothesis, in: **Journal of Development Studies**, 10, 66-78.

Harbison, S.F. (1981), Family Structure and Family Strategy in Migration Decision Making, in: G.F. De Jong and R.W. Gardner (eds.), **Migration Decision Making**, New York, etc., 225-251.

Harris, J.R. and M.P. Todaro (1970), Migration, Unemployment and Development: A Two-Sector Analysis, in: **American Economic Review**, 60, 126-142.

Heider, F. (1960), The Gestalt Theory of Motivation, in: M.R. Jones (ed.), **Nebraska Symposium on Motivation**, Lincoln, 145-172.

Hugo, G.J. (1981), Village-Community Ties, Village Norms and Ethnic and Social Networks: A Review of Evidence from the Third World, in: G.F. De Jong and F.W. Gardner (eds.), **Migration Decision Making**, New York, etc., 186-224.

Hunt, J.C. and J.B. Kau (1985), Migration and Wage Growth: A Human Capital Approach, in: **Southern Economic Journal**, 51, 697-710.

Johnson, G.E. (1971), The Structure of Rural-Urban Migration Models, in: **Eastern African Economic Review**, 3, 21-28.

Kahneman, D., P. Slovic and A. Tversky (eds.) (1982), **Judgement Under Uncertainty: Heuristics and Biases**, Cambridge etc.

Kahneman, D. and A. Tversky (1979), Prospect Theory: An Analysis of Decision under Risk, in: **Econometrica**, 47, 263-291.

——— (1982), Variants of Uncertainty, in: **Cognition**, 11, 143-157.

Knight, F.H. (1921), **Risk, Uncertainty, and Profit**, Cambridge.

Köhler, W. (1947), **Gestalt Psychology**, New York, 2. edition.

Krelle, W. (1957), Unsicherheit und Risiko in der Preisbildung, in: **Zeitschrift für die gesamte Staatswissenschaft**, 113, 632-677.

——— (1968), **Präferenz- und Entscheidungstheorie**, Tübingen.

Kunreuther, H., W. Sanderson and R. Vetschera (1985), A Behavioral Model of the Adoption of Protective Activities, in: **Journal of Economic Behavior and Organization**, 6, 1-15.

Lee, E.S. (1966), A Theory of Migration, in: **Demography**, 3, 47-57.

Leibenstein, H. (1963), **Economic Backwardness and Economic Growth**, New York.

Lubell, H. (1978), Urban Development and Employment: The Third World Metropolis, in: **International Labour Review**, 117, 747-756.

Lucas, R.E.B. (1985), Migration Amongst the Batswana, in: **Economic Journal**, 95, 358-382.

Mac Crimmon, K.R. and D.A. Wehrung (1986), **Taking Risks, The Management of Uncertainty**, New York-London.

Mac Donald, L.D. and J.S. Mac Donald (1969), Motives and Objectives of Migration: Selective Migration and Preferences Toward Rural and Urban Life, in: **Social and Economic Studies**, 17, 417-434.

Marshall, A. (1982), **Principles of Economics**, London-Basingstoke, 8. edition (Original 1890).

Metzger, W. (1931), Gestalt und Kontrast, in: **Psychologische Forschung**, 15, 374-386.

Mincer, J. (1978), Family Migration Decision, in: **Journal of Political Economy**, 86, 748-773.

Mitra, P.K. (1982), **A Theory of Interlinked Rural Transactions**, The World Bank Development Research Center, Discussion Papers No. 33.

Molho, I. (1986), Theories of Migration: A Review, in: **Scottish Journal of Political Economy**, 33, 396-419.

Pratt, J.W. (1964), Risk Aversion in the Small and in the Large, in: **Econometrica**, 32, 122-136.

Rapoport, A. (1987), **Die subjektiven Aspekte des Risikobegriffs**, Lecture at THD, 6.7.1987.

Röpke, J. (1977), **Die Strategie der Innovation**, Tübingen.

Schlicht, E. (1987), **Critique of a Custom in Labor Economics**, Darmstadt, unpublished mimeo.

Schneeweiß, H. (1967), **Entscheidungskriterien bei Risiko**, Berlin-Heidelberg-New York.

Schneider, D. (1980), **Investition und Finanzierung**, Wiesbaden, 5. edition.

Schubert, R. (1985), **Interne Migration in Entwicklungsländern**, Lecture at the section "Entwicklungsländer" in the Verein für Socialpolitik/Gesellschaft für Wirtschafts- und Sozialwissenschaften, Frankfurt/Main.

——— (1987), Interne Migration in Entwicklungsländern – Zur Rationalität von Land-Stadt-Wanderungen, in: **Zeitschrift für Wirtschaft- und Sozialwissenschaften**, 107, 207-223.

——— (1988a), **High Wages and Specific Reward Schedules** – On the Allocation of Risks Connected with Labour Relationships, Darmstadt, unpublished mimeo.

——— (1988b), Optimale Ausbeutung von Holz in der Republik Niger – zur Diskrepanz zwischen Theorie und Praxis, in: H. Körner (ed.), **Probleme der ländlichen Entwicklung in der dritten Welt**, Berlin.

Shaw, P.R. (1975), **Migration Theory and Fact**, Philadelphia.

Sethuraman, S.V. (1976), The Urban Informal Sector: Concept, Measurement and Policy, in: **International Labour Review**, 114, 69-81.

Simon, J.L. and J.A. Heins (1985), The Effect of Immigrants on Natives' Incomes Through the Use of Capital, in: **Journal of Development Economics**, 17, 75-93.

Sinn, H.-W. (1986), Risiko als Produktionsfaktor, in: **Jahrbücher für Nationalökonomie und Statistik**, 201, 557-571.

Speare Jr., A. (1971), A Cost-Benefit Model of Rural to Urban Migration in Taiwan, in: **Population Studies**, 25, 117-130.

Stark, O. (1985), Introduction, in: **Journal of Development Economics**, 17, 1-3.

Stark, O. and D. Levhari (1982), On Migration and Risk in LDCs, in: **Economic Development and Cultural Change**, 31, 191-196.

Stiglitz, J.E. (1974), Alternative Theories of Wage Determination and Unemployment in LDC 's: The Labor Turnover Model, in: **The Quarterly Journal of Economics**, 87, 194-227.

——— (1976), The Efficiency Wage Hypothesis, Surplus Labour, and the Distribution of Income in LDCs, in: **Oxford Economic Papers**, 28, 185-207.

Straubhaar, T. (1987), International Migration under Incomplete Information. A Comment, in: **Schweizerische Zeitschrift für Volkswirtschaft und Statistik**, 123, 219-226.

Tobin, J. (1958), Liquidity Preference as Behavior Towards Risk, in: **Review of Economic Studies**, 25, 65-86.

Todaro, M.P. (1969), A Model of Labor Migration and Urban Unemployment in Less Developed Countries, in: **American Economic Review**, 59, 138-148.

——— (1976), **Migration and Economic Development: A Review of Theory; Evidence, Methodology and Research Priorities**. Institute for Development Studies, University of Nairobi, Occasional Paper No. 18.

Tversky, A. and D. Kahneman (1981), The Framing of Decisions and the Psychology of Choice, in: **Science**, 211, 453-458.

Usher, D. (1977), Public Property and the Effects of Migration upon Other Residents of the Migrants Countries of Origin and Destination, in: **Journal of Political Economy**, 85, 1001-1020.

Wertheimer, M. (1945), **Productive Thinking**, New York-London.

Yellen, J.L. (1984), Efficiency Wage Models of Unemployment, in: **American Economic Review, Papers and Proceedings**, 74, 200-205.

Place of Birth and Past Place of Residence in South Korea: Methodological Considerations for Migration Research

Joachim Singelmann

Jiang Hong Li

Abstract: This paper evaluates the possibility to estimate immigration and net migration from information about place of birth by applying the census-survival-ratio (CSR) method to life-time migration. The results show that this procedure substantially underestimates actual immigration, especially in the young-adult ages. The procedure yields slightly better results with net migration, especially concerning the age profile. But this procedure is not a large improvement over estimates that can be obtained from applying the CSR method to the general population.

1. Introduction

Population distribution is increasingly becoming the major demographic concern of policy makers in developing countries. With the rates of overall population growth declining — albeit slowly — in many developing countries, their governments are turning their attention to the consequences of (1) *urbanization*, (2) the *urban system*, and (3) *regional population distribution* (Singelmann (1984); United Nations (1985)).

(1) With regard to urbanization, the concern is not with possible "overurbanization" but rather with the tempo or rate of urbanization. During the 1960s, especially in Latin America, many development specialists looked upon urbanization largely in negative terms (see Morse (1965)). Their view was that the level of urbanization in Latin American countries — but also elsewhere — was above what was "appropriate" for their level of industrialization, thus representing overurbanization. Subsequent studies (e.g. United Nations (1980)), however, did not find any evidence for such wholesale indictment of urbanization, so that today overurbanization is no longer an important matter of concern. However, even if the level of urbanization, by historical standards, appears to be in line with industrialization, the very pace of urbanization is of concern to policy makers, for it creates tremendous demands for urban resources. This is especially the case in countries where the urban natural increase is high to begin with; in these countries urban population growth from rapid urbanization is added to high urban population due to the natural increase of the urban population.

(2) The concern with the urban system is largely related to the frequently high degree of concentration of the urban population in one large city in many developing countries. To the extent that rapid urbanization puts pressure on the resources available in developing countries, these pressures intensify the more the urban system tends towards *primacy*, i.e. where urbanization mostly takes place in one or two large cities. As in the case of the general urban population, these cities are often already exhibiting high rates of population growth from the natural increase of the native population

(see Singelmann (1984)). Moreover, the absolute size of many of the largest cities in developing countries makes them increasingly difficult to manage administratively.

(3) The high primacy of the urban system in many developing countries usually goes hand in hand with a regional population concentration often leading to large urban-rural and regional disparities in terms of social and economic development. These disparities are reflected, among other things, in higher urban life expectancy and higher per capita income in the region in which the primate city (very often the political capital) is located. For these reasons, policies aimed at decentralization and polarization reversal have been recommended to many developing countries and several (e.g. Mexico and South Korea) have begun to implement such policies. And many countries have taken an interest in policies aimed at the development of small and intermediate size cities (Richardson (1984); see also United Nations Fund for Population Activities (1986)).

All three areas of concern — urbanization, urban system, and regional population distribution — are intimately linked to migration. Notwithstanding some rural-urban differentials in natural increase, the major source for urbanization is rural-to-urban migration (United Nations (1980)). Similarly, the differential growth of cities and regions comes about mostly as a result of selected migration to the large cities and regions that offer economic opportunities and social mobility.

Given this linkage between migration and urbanization, primate urban development and regional population concentration, information about the rate and composition of migration, among other aspects, is essential for policy makers. Without knowing who the immigrants and outmigrants are and what the rate is at which they are entering and departing cities, it is difficult to plan and provide the urban and social services required by migrants.

Information about internal (as well as international) migration, however, is not as readily available as that about birth and deaths, for which registration systems exist in many countries; those registrations then are made publicly available as part of the official statistics. Migratory moves, on the other hand, generally go unrecorded, for they are considered to be private decisions without legal ramifications (e.g. identity cards upon births or inheritance upon death). Even where population registers exist and/or where people have to report their residence to local administrations, that information typically is not publicly available. Thus, the main source of knowledge about internal migration is the population census. That information is generally obtained through a question about a person's residence n-number of years ago (usually five years ago) or length of residence at the present residence. By comparing previous residence with current residence, it is then possible to estimate average annual rates of migration during that time interval.

While an increasing number of developing countries now follows international guidelines to include into their census schedules questions about residence n-number of year ago, for many developing countries place of birth is often the only information on previous residence; this limitation is especially widespread in African countries.

In the absence of information on previous residence n-number of years ago, researchers have thus had to rely on place of birth as their sole information about migration streams. Any persons born in a different place (city, county, state, region etc.) than the place of their current residence are considered life-time migrants. The use of the concept of life-time migration for the estimation of the volume of migration is problematic, however, that one does not have any information as to when the migration took place. The older the life-time migrant is, the more could his or her migration be in the past. It is therefore impossible to estimate migration rates for a specific time period if the only information available is life-time migration at one point in time.

For an increasing number of developing countries, however, there are now two censuses available which contain information on place of residence by age. This has led to suggestions that the use of the *census survival ratio* method might make it possible to estimate actual migration flows during the intercensal period from information about life-time migration.

The main purpose of this paper is to assess the possibility to use information about place of birth for the estimation of migration rates. If it can be shown that place of birth yields acceptable estimates of migration for a specific time period, much more could be learned about migration in those countries where that type of information about residence is the only source available about nationwide migration.

2. Data and Methods

2.1 Data

We chose South Korea for our comparison of the various migration estimates, because it is one of the very few developing countries for which the past two censuses asked about place of birth and place of residence five years ago. Usually countries obtain either place-of-birth or past-residence information. Moreover, the South Korean census publishes that information by age and sex, which is essential for the estimation technique. South Korea offers additional advantages for the purposes of this study: (1) its census data are of high quality guaranteeing some reliability of the results; and (2) it also asked the less common question about place of residence one year ago; this allows an assessment of how many migrants might not stay for the full five year period that is the basis for the usual estimates of migration.

We will thus examine three sources of information about migration: place of residence five years ago; place of birth; and place of residence one year ago. In addition, we shall present estimates of migration obtained from an application of census survival ratios to the general population in specific regions.

Our data come from the 1970 and 1980 census of population for South Korea. We used the residence questions to compute immigration and outmigration for every region in South Korea except

Jeju (which is a small island in the South).[1] Crosslisting current and previous residence (or place of birth), we computed for each region the number of immigrants and outmigrants by age and sex.[2] We will estimate migration separately for males and females because of the generally different rates and age profile of migration for men and women.

2.2. Method

Our estimate of migration for the period 1970-80 from information about life-time migration is derived from the following procedure. Define for each sex separately:

T(i,1) = population size in age interval i (assumed to be five years wide) at the initial census;

T(i,2) = population size in age interval i at the second census, 10 years later;

LM(i,1), LM(i,2) = life-time immigrants in age interval i at the first and second census.

The steps in the procedure then are the following:

(1) Calculate "cohort survival" rates for the total population:

---

1 We excluded Jeju for two reasons: (1) it is so small that its magnitude of migration is minimal compared to the other regions; and (2) being an island we believe that it would not be comparable to the other regions.

2 We excluded those who were born abroad and those for whom previous residence was unknown. The former are international migrants rather than internal migrants; the category "unknown" is very small and would not change the results.

$$S(i) = \frac{T(i+2,2)}{T(i,1)}$$

(2) Apply the cohort survival rates to the appropriate life-time-*immigrant* cohorts at time 1 to derive the predicted number of urban persons in this cohort 10 years, hence:

$$PLM(i+2,2) = S(i)*LM(i,1);$$

(3) Subtract the predicted number of life-time migrants from the actual number of life-time migrants to derive an estimate of surviving *immigrants* during the period 1970-80:

$$NSM(i+2,2) = LM(i+2,2) - PLM(i+2,2)$$

The estimated number of migrants for the period 1970-80 thus is the number of 1980 life-time immigrants minus the number of 1970 life-time immigrants that could be expected to survive until 1980. In order to make the two time periods comparable, we multiplied the number of actual immigrants by 2, thus assuming no change in the volume of immigration during the 1970s.

We performed the estimations for all regions and found no major differences in the fit of estimated and actual migration. For the sake of clarity of presentation, we are therefore showing the results for six regions. We selected the following regions for presentation: Seoul, Busan, Gyeonggi, Gyeongsangbug, Gyeongsangnam and Jeonnam. Seoul and Busan are mostly urban regions containing the two largest South Korean cities. Their level of development is much higher than the South Korean average. Gyeonggi is the region surrounding Greater Seoul. The recent decentralization efforts of South Korea aimed at shifting industrialization away from Seoul towards Gyeonggi, and it is beginning to show some effects. The per capita income of Gyeonggi is about the same as the South Korean average. The other three regions selected represent the more rural and less developed parts of South Korea.[3] Given the general finding about a positive relationship among regions between level of development and immigration, we thus should expect net immigration in Seoul, Busan and Gyeonggi and net outmigration in the other three regions.

We made one further refinement of the census survival method. Since the six regions differ in their levels of development, it should be expected that the life expectancy and mortality rates in these regions differ as well. While we do not have region-specific information about these factors, we decided to apply the following weights to the census survival ratios: 1.15 for Seoul and Busan, 1.0 for Gyeonggi, and .85 for Jeonnam. We thus assumed that the mortality rates in Seoul and Busan were 15 percent lower than the national average, and that they were 15 percent higher in Gyeongsangbug, Gyeongsangnam, and Jeonnam. The mortality rates for Gyeonggi were assumed to be the same as the national average. The 15-percent difference in the mortality rates implies that the life expectancy in Seoul and Busan is about 3 years more than that for South Korea as a whole, whereas it is about 3 years less in Jeonnam. These assumptions are consistent with those made by

3 Since 1980, however, those areas have had an above average rate of population growth and urbanization.

Preston (1979) and the United Nations (1980), (1985) in comparable studies of migration and natural increase in developing countries.

For these six regions, we present three kinds of comparisons: (a) immigration on the basis of place of residence five years ago versus immigration from information about place of birth; (b) immigration on the basis of place of residence five years ago *versus* immigration on the basis of place of residence one year ago; and (c) net migration estimated from information about residence five years ago, life-time migration and overall population change. We now turn to the first set of comparison.

3. Actual and Estimated Inmigration 1970-80

Figures 1 and 2 present actual and estimated immigration to the six provinces during 1970-80 for males and females. Actual immigration is based on a cross-classification of current place of residence by place of residence five years ago. We classified those persons as immigrants who in 1975 did not reside in the region in which they were enumerated in 1980. Estimated immigration is obtained from the method outlined above.

The results of these estimates (see Figures 1 and 2) show that in all regions and for both males and females, the estimates of immigration fall below the actual immigration. For Seoul, Busan, and Gyeonggi, the estimated volume of male immigration during the period 1970-80 falls short of the actual volume of immigration by 25-40 percent; the underestimation is even worse for Gyeongsangbug, Gyeongsangnam, and Jeonnam, ranging from 50-75 percent. The ratio of total estimated to total actual immigration is

Figure 1:

Actual and Estimated Male Immigration, 1970-80

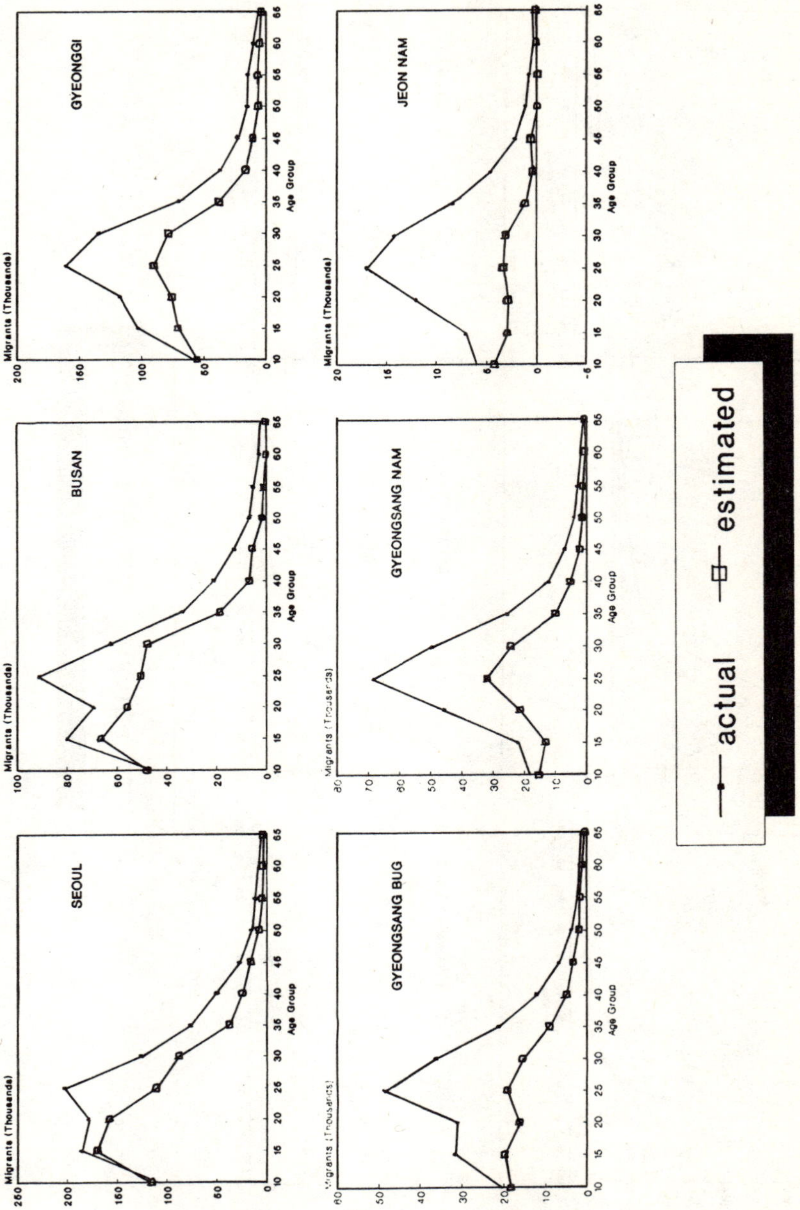

Figure 2:

Actual and Estimated Female Immigration, 1970-80

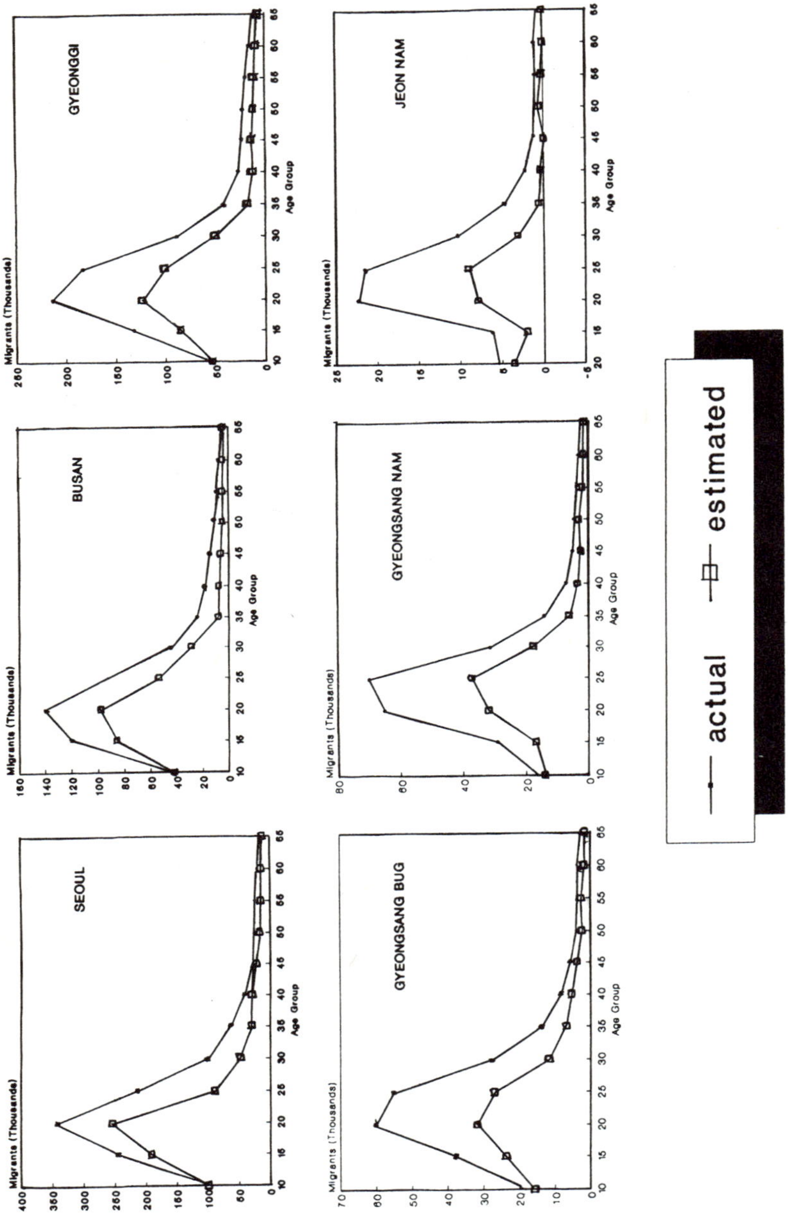

similar for females. Moreover, the underestimation is especially pronounced in the ages 15-39 (and sometimes also for older ages). Thus, the estimates of immigration derived from life-time migration fall far below the actual number. Moreover, the underestimation, while applying to most ages, is especially concentrated in the young-adult ages; the estimates therefore also do not represent the age structure of actual immigration.

We believe that the main reason for this shortcoming is the fact that the information about life-time migration does not allow the estimation of life-time immigrants in 1970 who decided to leave the region during the 1970s. By ignoring the 1970 life-time immigrants who subsequently leave the region, we expect too many 1970 life-time immigrants to survive through 1980 and thus underestimate the total number of 1970-80 immigrants. As Figures 1 and 2 show, this estimation error is particularly large for those age groups that account for most migrants, i.e. the ages with the highest rates of migration.[4]

4 We tried to estimate the outmigration of persons during the period 1970-80 who were life-time inmigrants in 1970. We first estimated outmigration with the same technique as reported here for inmigration. We then assumed that the outmigration rate of the general population could be applied to the outmigration of persons who were previously inmigrants. That assumption lead to a substantial overestimation in inmigration. We have not yet completed all our analyses of estimation the outmigration and/or return migration of previous life-time inmigrants, but we doubt that we can arrive at a reasonably stable weight of the rate of outmigration across regions to improve the overall estimation.

4. Immigration 1975-80

The 1980 census for South Korea also permitted a comparison of the volume of migration derived from information about place of residence one year and five years ago. For both cases, we classified those persons as immigrants who in 1979 or in 1975 did not reside in the region in which they were enumerated in 1980. If we assume that the volume of immigration did not change during the period 1975-80, the number of immigrants during that period obtained from information about residence five years ago should equal five times the number of migrants during that period obtained from information about residence one year ago.

The estimation results are presented in Figure 3 for males and Figure 4 for females. These figures show that the number of migrants estimated from the information about residence in 1979 exceeds the volume of migration estimated from information about residence five years ago. For both males and females, total immigration on the basis of the 1979 residence exceeds the estimate derived from the 1975 residence: by about one-third in Busan and 60-80 percent in Seoul, Gyeonggi, Gyeongsangbug, and Gyeongsangnam. The two estimates are closest for Jeonnam, where the 1979-estimate is only 20 percent larger than the 1975-estimate for male and 7 percent for females. Again, the differences between the two estimates are especially large for those age groups that are typical for migrants (i.e. ages 15-34).

There are several explanations for the differing estimation results. First, immigration could have accelerated during the period 1975-80. In that case, the multiplication of the 1979-80 migration

Figure 3:

Male Immigration by Age, 1970-80

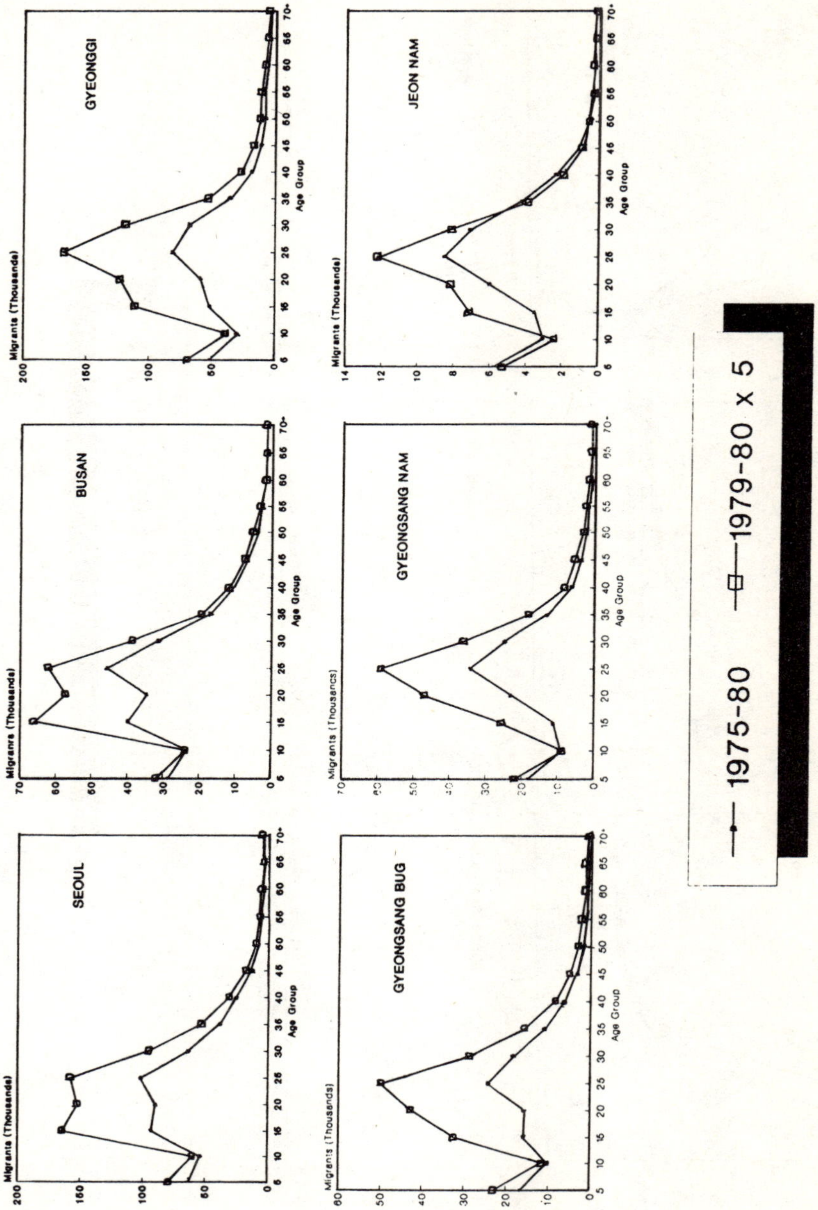

Figure 4:

Female Immigration by Age, 1970-80

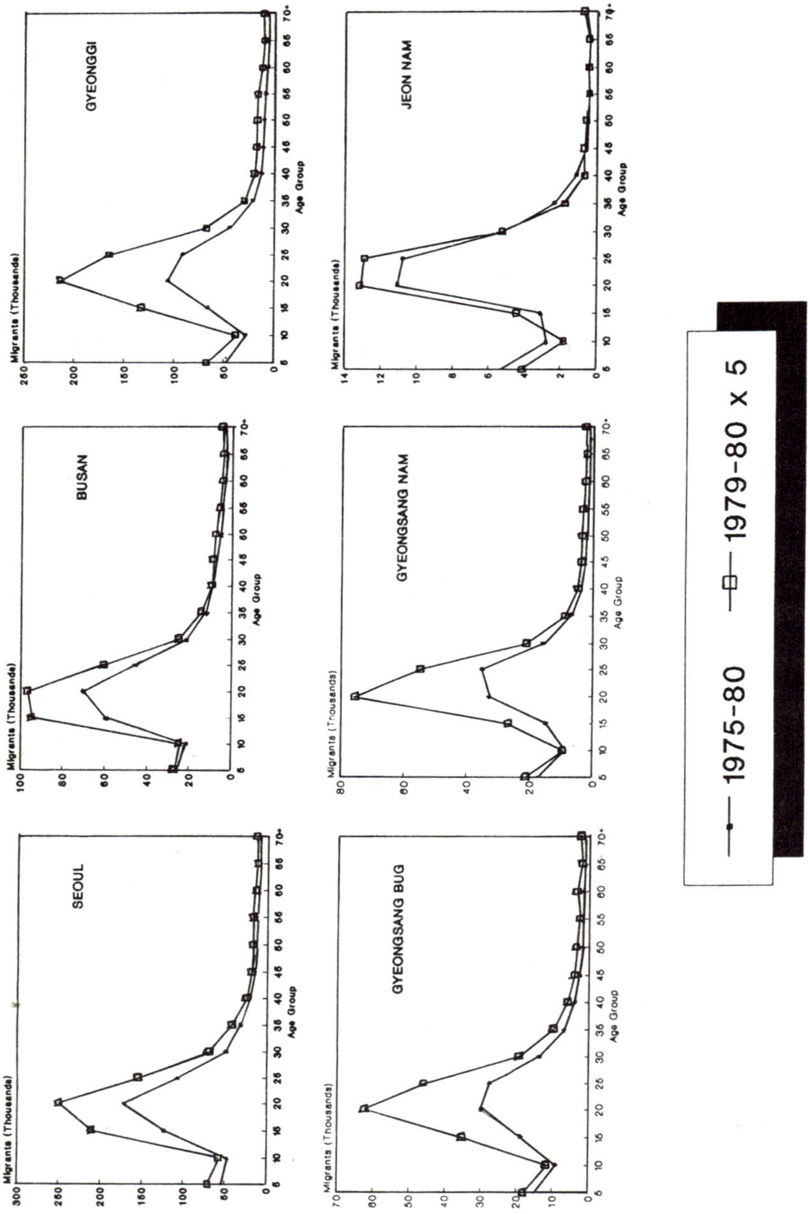

by five would have led to an overestimation. We do not think, however, that this explains the estimation differences, for there is no indication that immigration accelerated during the late 1970s, at least not in the case of Seoul and Busan. The decentralization policies of South Korea are more likely to have slowed the immigration to those two urban regions (see also United Nations (1980), (1985)). Moreover, if immigration really accelerated during the late 1970s, the number of immigrants estimated from the 1979 residence should exceed the number of immigrants estimated from the 1975 residence at all ages. But the differences are largely concentrated in the age range of 15-34 years of age.

Second, the number of migrants estimated from the 1979 residence will exceed that estimated from the 1975 residence if some migrants who moved into the region after 1975 leave the region prior to 1980. A five-year time period is more likely than a one-year period to include those immigrants who subsequently become outmigrants. Since the estimation differences apply mostly to the age groups during which persons tends to migrate, this second possibility appears to be the better explanation for the differences shown in Figures 3 and 4.

If that explanation is correct, it also suggests, however, that the number of migrants estimated from the 1975 residence is not an underestimation of the total immigrants present in 1980. Rather, the information about the 1975 residence yields an estimate of the total number of immigrants during the period 1975-80 who remained in the region and survived through 1980. The information about the 1979 residence, on the other hand, yields an estimate of the total volume of immigrants during the period 1975-70, regardless of whether they actually stayed in that region during the period. For policy purposes, both types of information are important.

5. Actual and Estimated Net Migration

Our final comparison concerns different estimations of net migration. Given the previously made observation that the data for life-time migration do not permit the estimation of 1970 life-time immigrants who leave the region of immigration during the intercensal period, we decided to estimate the number of net migrants during the period 1970-80, using the same procedure as outlined above. (In this case, however, we applied the census survival ratios to net life-time migrants rather than immigrants.) The actual number of net migrants was obtained from the information about residence in 1975.

The levels of actual net migration and estimated net migration based on place of birth (EST-LIFE) are presented in Figures 5 and 6. The results show that the estimates of the volume of net migration differs from the actual volume of net migration, but the difference tends to be smaller than in the case of immigration, especially for Seoul, Busan, and Gyeonggi. On the other hand, the estimated net migration for Gyeongsangnam grossly overestimates the net outmigration from that region. In contrast to immigration, however, the age profiles of actual and estimated net migration are more similar (excepting Gyeongsangnam). Thus, with respect to net migration, the procedure to estimate migration for a specific time period from information about place of birth yields results that more closely fit the actual levels and age profile of net migration.

Figure 5:

Actual and Estimated Male Net Migration, 1970-80

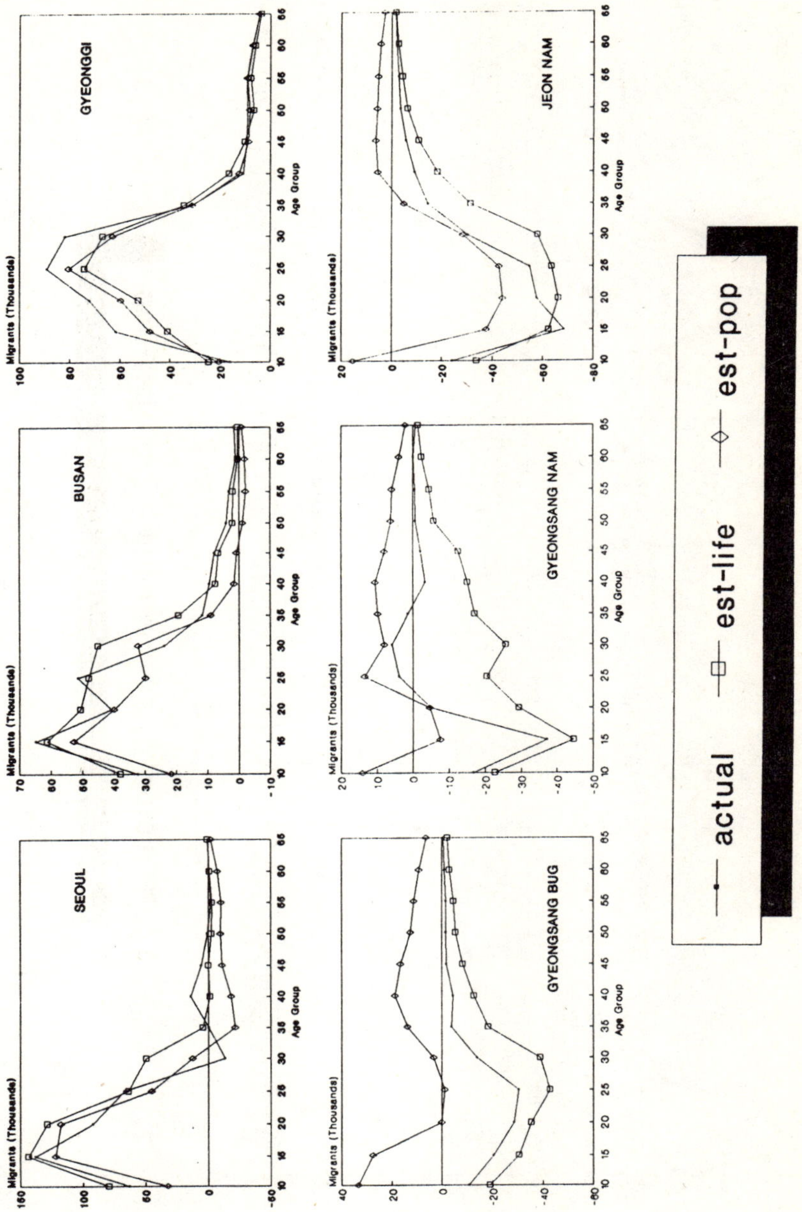

Figure 6:

Actual and Estimated Female Net Migration, 1970-80

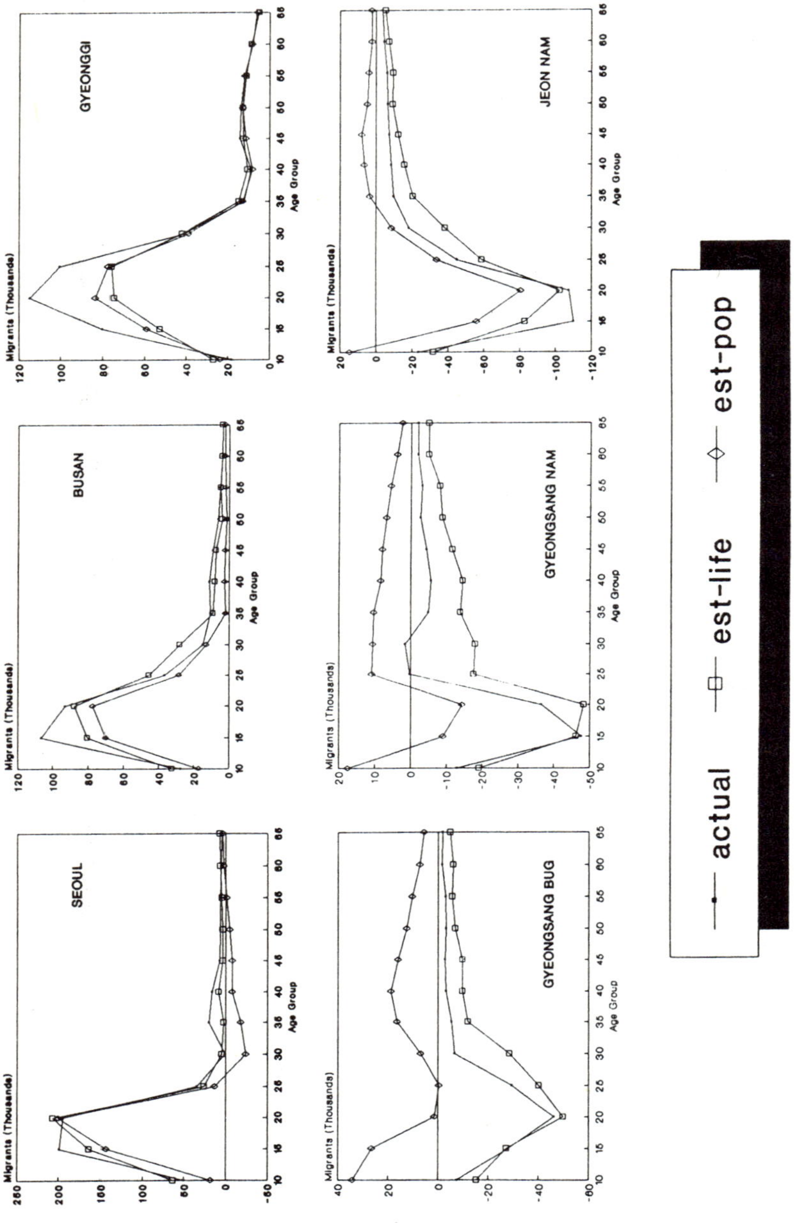

However, as Figures 5 and 6 show, almost the same fit can be obtained by applying the census survival rate to the 1970 population in each region. While the resulting estimated volume of net migration based on the total regional population (EST-POP) is not as similar to actual net migration as are the estimates based on life-time migration, that difference is not particularly large. Also, the age profile of estimated net migration (EST-POP) resembles the age profile of actual net migration. Since age-sex specific information on place of birth is often not available, whereas regional population figures are commonly tabulated by age and sex, the EST-POP estimates of net migration thus can be used almost as well as the EST-LIFE estimates to represent actual net migration.

6. Conclusion

Our results suggest that place of birth is no substitute for information about place of residence x-number of years ago, even when this information is available for two censuses. Estimates of immigration based on place of birth tend to grossly understate regional immigration. Furthermore, while information about place of birth permits fair estimates of the volume of net migration and good representations of its age structure, it is not a substantial improvement over the estimates of net migration that can be more readily obtained from an application of census survival ratios to regional population change. In sum, the hopes that the wave of 1980-round censuses with information about place of birth will enable us to gain more insights into the recent migration process in these countries do not appear to be warranted.

References

Morse, R. (1965), Recent Research on Latin American Urbanization: A Selective Survey with Commentary, in: **Latin American Research Review**, 1.

Preston, S.H. (1979), Urban Growth in Developing Countries: A Demographic Reappraisal, in: **Population and Development Review**, 5, 195-215.

Richardson, H.W. (1984), Population Distribution Policies," in: United Nations (ed.) **Population Distribution, Migration and Development**. United Nations, New York.

Singelmann, J. (1984), Migration and the Growth of Metropolitan Areas of the Third World, in: R.F. Tomasson (ed.) **Comparative Social Research**, 7. CT: Jai Press, Greenwich.

——— (),Verstädterung, Wanderung und Beschäftigung in Entwicklungsländern, in: G. Steinmann, K.F. Zimmermann, and G. Heilig (eds.) **Probleme und Chancen demographischer Entwicklung in der Dritten Welt**. Springer Verlag, Berlin.

United Nations (1980), **Patterns of Urban and Rural Population Growth**. United Nations, New York.

——— (1985), **Migration, Population Growth and Employment in Metropolitan Areas of Selected Developing Countries**. United Nations, New York.

——— (1985), **World Population Trends, Population and Development Interrelations and Population Policies - 1983 Monitoring Report**. United Nations, New York.

United Nations Fund for Population Activities (1986), **Declaración de Mexico sobre Población y Ciudades Pequeñas y Medianas en America Latina y el Caribe**. New York.

V. Immigration Policy

Migration Pressure in Germany: Past and Future*

Christoph M. Schmidt

Klaus F. Zimmermann

Abstract: This paper investigates the West German experience with immigration after World War II. It is argued that West Germany has been an immigration country ever since the beginning of the fifties. The size of the inflow of migrants is comparable to the population pressure to the USA at the beginning of the century. From this perspective, the dramatic tone of the current migration debate in Europe is qualified. The view taken is more optimistic: Even if larger immigration takes place, it might be beneficial from an economic point of view. Also, it will compensate for the stagnating population due to low (below replacement) fertility rates.

1. Introduction

This paper evaluates the past and the prospective migration experience of Germany as a model case for the entirety of Central

---

* This paper is a substantial revision of an invited lecture the second author has given at the conference "Underdevelopment and Migration", February 14-16, 1991 in Verona. We wish to thank Stefan Hochgürtel and Anja Koch for able research assistance.

European countries. It is demonstrated that migrant inflow into Germany has been substantial already since the 1950s, both in absolute and in relative terms. Taking into account the idiosyncrasies generated by German re-unification and by the presence of large numbers of ethnic Germans in East Europe, it is argued that the integration potential of the German economy is large, even in the face of the massive immigration flows that are expected for the near future. From this perspective, we qualify the dramatic tone of the current migration debate in Europe.

In section 2, we review the problems of ageing societies and of the integration of large migration inflows with respect to their present importance for European labor markets. Using current data, it is shown that the situation of Germany is representative for other European countries in many respects. In section 3, we examine Germany's post-war immigration history and distinguish several immigration regimes. Section 4 evaluates this experience with a focus on the revealed integration potential of the German economy and uses our conclusions to infer on future developments. In the final section 5, we discuss these results from a European perspective.

2. Europe's Problems and Germany's Model Role

There are two dominant problems for the European labor markets at the dawn of the 21st century. First, there is the overall trend of population ageing in Central Europe caused by persistent below replacement fertility rates. Taken by itself, this development will create a vacuum on the labor markets by the turn of the century, and hence population demand pull. Second, there is a large migration potential of individuals from low-income countries from the East and from the South. These countries have both considerably younger populations and excess supply on their labor markets. The pressure exerted by them will take two basic forms. They will either lobby to be accepted as member states into the European Community or they will try to acquire the right of free mobility into the Community for their citizens. The magnitude of this migration potential clearly exceeds the potential induced by the de-regulation of the European Community's labor markets for current EC citizens.

While the inflow of young migrants might be an immediate remedy for the European ageing problem, it might well be that the social cost for the receiving countries outweigh the economic gains from migration. Even worse, it might be that virtually no gains are generated at all if migrants are consistently of low value to the receiving labor market. Unfortunately, a solid assessment of the situation is precluded as of yet by a lack of knowledge about these economic consequences.

Furthermore, policy makers seem to value the fear that migration will cause social tensions in the immigration countries so high as to disengage from rational discussions of the issue. For instance, the German government seeks to avoid these by stating that *Germany is no immigration country*. It will be argued in this paper that this view is not only counterfactual, but that it also overlooks the need for a coordinating migration policy that could fruitfully incorporate the interests of both emigration and immigration countries.

In fact, it turns out that Germany is able to serve as a model case for other potential immigration countries in Central Europe. It has a long and intense migration history, a high share of foreigners and foreign workers and it promises to be a very attractive destination for future migrants. The first of these three points is generally underrated in the public debate and will be discussed in depth in this paper. The latter points are easily demonstrated.

Germany's position as one of the European countries with a high share of foreigners among both the population and the work force is reported for the year 1988 in Table 1. Columns 1 to 3 show for all 12 EC member states the population size, the size of the foreign population, and the number of foreign workers, respectively. Column 4 reports the number of foreign workers originating from other EC member states. West Germany, France and the United Kingdom have the largest absolute numbers of foreigners and foreign workers.

To make these figures comparable, the raw numbers are weighted by the respective population size. With respect to the share of foreigners in the total population, the sequence is Luxemburg 25.8 %, Belgium 8.6%, West Germany 7.3%, France 5.0%, The Netherlands 3.8%, United Kingdom 3.0%, Denmark 2.5%, Greece 1.9 %, Portugal 0.9%, Spain 0.9%, and Italy 0.8%. The ranking of the first six countries according to the share of foreign workers in the total population is Luxemburg 15.7%, West Germany 2.6%, France 2.1%, Belgium 1.9%, United Kingdom 1.4%, and The Netherlands 1.2%. Ranking the countries according to the share of foreign workers from EC countries or the share of foreign workers from non-EC countries in the total population, Germany would be 4th and 1st, respectively.

Table 1:

Population Size and Foreigners in EC Countries (1988)

In Thousands

	Population (1)	Foreigners (2)	Workers Foreign (3)	Workers EC (4)
Belgium	9884	853.2[b]	187.0	140.8
Denmark	5130	128.3[b]	45.5	12.4
West Germany	61451	4489.1	1577.1	472.7
France	55884	2785.0[a]	1172.5	589.3
United Kindom	57065	1736.0[c]	820.9	398.2
Greece	10010	193.4	24.9	6.6
Ireland	3538	—	19.9	16.1
Italy	57441	429.4[d]	57.0	14.0
Luxemburg	375	96.8[b]	58.8	55.9
The Netherlands	14760	568.0[b]	175.7	86.2
Portugal	10305	89.8[b]	30.5	6.8
Spain	38809	354.9	57.0	22.0

Table 1: continued

In Per Cent

	(2):(1)	(3):(1)	(4):(1)
Belgium	8.6	1.9	1.4
Denmark	2.5	0.9	0.2
West Germany	7.3	2.6	0.8
France	5.0	2.1	1.1
United Kingdom	3.0	1.4	0.7
Greece	1.9	0.3	0.1
Ireland	—	0.6	0.5
Italy	0.8	0.1	0.0
Luxemburg	25.8	15.7	14.9
The Netherlands	3.8	1.2	0.6
Portugal	0.9	0.3	0.1
Spain	0.9	0.2	0.1

Source: Population (middle of the year): OECD, Main Economic Indicators, 1991. Foreigners: Statistisches Bundesamt, Statistisches Jahrbuch für das Ausland, 1990. Foreign Workers and EEC workers: Statistisches Bundesamt, Statistik des Auslands, 1990.

[a] Statistisches Bundesamt, Länderbericht Frankreich, 1989.

[b] 1987

[c] 1985

[d] 1981

Germany will remain an attractive destination for future migrants. Even after the unification of both Germanies, the now larger country satisfies most of the key necessary criteria to be a typical immigration country: High economic growth, comparatively low unemployment rates, low inflation (though at a higher rate in 1991), an attractive social security system, low (below replacement) fertility rates, and, as a consequence, a rapidly ageing society with the need to either compensate this by higher fertility, higher labor productivity or a larger amount of immigration.

It is for these reasons that some German newspapers have recently received attention when they claimed that there might soon be a flow of some forty million migrants from the East. More serious speculations predict an East-West migration wave of permanent or temporary migrants of about five million people. Germany, Austria, France, Italy and the Benelux countries will most likely be the receiving countries of this immigrant stream. Other parts of West Europe, however, will probably be affected, too.

Clearly, the past and the prospective immigration experience of each European country will have some idiosyncratic elements, for example because of ties to former colonies that are now members of the Third World. The German situation has to be qualified for two reasons. Unification has changed the picture somewhat due to the fact that East Germany had no significant immigration. Unified Germany thus mixes the history of a country that integrated substantial numbers of foreigners into the population and its work force with the history of a country virtually new to the phenomenon of immigration.

On the other hand, a large part of immigration to West Germany after World War II was an inflow of East Germans or of individuals of German origin, and thus is not counted in a comparison as in Table 1. That is, if these individuals were to a certain extent comparable to foreign immigrants, these calculations would understate the actual integration requirements that Germany has faced and mastered in the past. We would indeed argue that nationality considerations were of small importance and that Germans moving to Germany posed a considerable integration problem to the German economy. These individuals should therefore be treated as migrants in the analysis.

Independent of our decision about this issue, West Germany has to be seen among the countries with the largest immigration experience in Europe from the guestworker figures alone. Together with Germany's attractiveness to future migrants, this already indicates that Germany could serve as a benchmark case in the current European migration debate. The rest of the paper will be devoted to a deeper discussion of Germany's immigration history. This discussion will lend more support to our conclusion that Germany has a long and intense immigration experience. In fact, we view the Federal Republic of Germany as an immigration country during most of its existence.

In particular, we will argue that Germany had to integrate a migrant flow whose magnitude has been on the order of the inflow to other countries commonly accepted as typical immigration countries. This argument is exemplified using the case of the United States during its own period of the highest relative migrant inflow at the beginning of this century. We will start in the next section with a more descriptive analysis, outlining four distinct phases in the period from 1950 to 1990: (a) the *War Adjustment Phase*, (b) the *Manpower Recruitment Phase*, (c) the *Consolidation Phase*, and (d) the *German-German Migration Phase*. These migration flows will then be evaluated in the following section and the resulting migration pressure will be shown to be mostly comparable to the immigration pressure experienced by the United States during the period from 1901 to 1910.

3. Post-War Migration Flows

This section provides a description of the West German immigration experience after World War II. It is shown that Germany's post-war history is usefully partitioned into four distinct phases and that this country has experienced net immigration over most of its existence. Special attention is given to the distinction of the immigrants into East Germans, ethnic Germans migrating from abroad, and foreigners, and to the relative share of these groups in the immigration flow.

Migration is not a new issue for Germany. It is only a feature of more recent decades, however, that it has been a receiving country. There was a large amount of emigration from Germany in the 19th century as Germany was relatively late to industrialize. Three large emigration waves to the United States took place: 5.1 million Germans moved to the USA from 1820 to 1910. However, from the beginning of the 20th century until World War I, also 1 million European immigrants came to Germany as a consequence of the population demand caused by Germany's own industrialization process.

Since World War II, the migration flows to West Germany mainly exceeded the corresponding emigration flows. Up to 1950, about 12 million Germans had to leave East Europe. About 8 millions of them came to West Germany. At the same time, a considerable amount of Germans emigrated, mainly to the United States, although the number of emigrants was smaller than that of immigrants by an order of magnitude. Since then, emigration has been moderate. Starting in 1950, four distinct phases can be identified, (a) the *War Adjustment Phase* from 1950 to August 13, 1961, the day of the building of the Berlin wall, (b) the *Manpower Recruitment Phase* from August 1961 to November 1973, (c) the *Consolidation Phase* from 1974 to 1988, and (d) the *German-German Migration Phase* from 1989, including November 9, 1989, the day of the fall of the Berlin wall and the breakdown of the inner German border, to October 3, 1990, the day of German re-unification.

In the analysis of these migration waves, one has to differentiate between three categories of migrants: foreigners, "Aussiedler", and "Übersiedler". The main distinction between these categories is the citizenship status. Foreigners, naturally, are not German citizens and their right to migrate to Germany is, in principle, subject to regulation. "Übersiedler" are Germans from the German Democratic Republic (GDR, East Germany) who were leaving the GDR to live permanently in the Federal Republic of Germany (FRG, West Germany). This migrant category ceased to exist with German re-unification. The German constitution ("Grundgesetz") considered all citizens of the GDR as well as the West Germans themselves as German citizens, and thus, in particular, the "Übersiedler". "Aussiedler" are repatriated persons, German nationals or people of German origin who leave their emigration areas in East Europe to move to the FRG. They are also viewed as German citizens. Due to their German citizenship, any limitation on their mobility to Germany is precluded.

In other aspects, however, from the viewpoint of social and cultural differences and from the viewpoint of integrability into the German labor market, the three migrant categories share a lot of problems. "Übersiedler" and "Aussiedler" mostly speak German and have a cultural tradition similar to West Germans. But depending on their place of origin when emigrating the differences can be substantial and, indeed, they seem to have grown, the later migration waves are studied. For instance, among recent "Übersiedler" cohorts, knowledge of German is no longer certain.

We would even argue that Germans originating in the countries of East Europe might be harder to integrate into the German labor market than workers from the fairly industrialized market economies in Europe's South, despite language barriers. In conclusion, in an analysis of the migration pressure exerted by immigrant inflow into Germany, the distinct migrant groups should be treated alike. Thus our focus will lie on the sum of migrant inflows.

In Table 2 the annual development of the West German population, including individuals with and without German citizenship, is shown together with the respective figures of gross and net

Table 2:

Population Size, Gross and Net Immigration

in Thousands

Year	Population[a]	Immigration	
		Gross	Net
War Adjustment Phase			
1950	47 695.7[b]	550.7	378.0
1951	50 336.1	386.2	137.6
1952	50 726.0	312.4	64.9
1953	51 051.9	500.3	348.8
1954	51 639.6	410.4	221.1
1955	52 126.8	501.7	333.3
1956	52 698.3	561.9	348.2
1957	53 318.8	648.2	400.8
1958	53 993.8	539.6	305.0
1959	54 606.0	434.8	170.9
1960	55 123.4	659.5	335.8
1961	55 784.8	742.2	419.2
Manpower Recruitment Phase			
1962	56 589.1	607.4	283.3
1963	57 247.2	646.3	223.5
1964	57 864.5	763.7	301.5
1965	58 587.5	839.9	343.8
1966	59 296.6	745.7	131.6
1967	59 792.9	431.8	-176.9
1968	59 948.5	686.1	278.3
1969	60 463.0	1012.2	572.0
1970	61 194.6	1072.4	575.2
1971	61 001.2	987.7	430.3
1972	61 502.5	903.1	330.5
1973	61 809.4	967.9	384.0

Table 2: continued

in Thousands

Year	Population[a]	Immigration Gross	Immigration Net
Consolidation Phase			
1974	62 101.4	629.8	-9.3
1975	61 991.5	456.1	-199.4
1976	61 644.6	498.7	-72.3
1977	61 442.0	539.9	32.7
1978	61 352.7	575.9	115.4
1979	61 321.7	666.7	246.0
1980	61 439.3	753.4	311.9
1981	61 657.9	625.1	152.4
1982	61 712.7	420.8	-71.9
1983	61 546.1	372.0	-115.3
1984	61 306.7	457.1	-145.7
1985	61 049.3	509.3	89.4
1986	61 020.5	596.7	195.9
1987	61 140.5	614.6	220.0
1988	61 238.1	903.9	485.6
German-German Migration Phase			
1989	61 715.1	1522.2	977.2

Source: Statistisches Bundesamt: Fachserie 1, Reihe 1, Bevölkerung und Erwerbstätigkeit; Statistisches Jahrbuch; Wirtschaft und Statistik, various issues.

[a] At the beginning of the year

[b] September 13, 1950.

immigration for the time from 1950 to 1989, separated into four panels. The first panel documents the *War Adjustment Phase* (1950 - August 13, 1961). This period was dominated by the exodus of 2.6 million Germans from the German Democratic Republic to the Federal Republic of Germany. The construction of the Berlin Wall and of a fence through Germany stopped this movement essentially altogether. In total, gross immigration has been 6.25 million people and net immigration has been 3.46 million people.

During this period, the population size was rising from about 48 million to roughly 56 million people, and unemployment was steadily decreasing. The unemployment rates in the first part of the 1950s were very high, 10.4% in 1950 and 5.2% in 1955. However, an increasing labor demand caused by the "economic miracle" changed this substantially at the end of the decade. In 1962, the unemployment rate was 1.2%. This improved the speed of the economic integration of migrants considerably. In 1960, there were already rising tensions in the labor market due to a shortage of labor, which had to be compensated by foreign labor.

In the *Manpower Recruitment Phase* (August 1961 - November 1973) that is reported in the second panel of Table 2, the shortage of labor which was no longer compensated by the inflow of people of German origin, induced a search for cheap foreign labor. A *Guest Worker System* was established by means of a series of recruitment treaties with Italy (1955), Spain and Greece (1960), Turkey (1961), Portugal (1964), and Yugoslavia (1968). There were about 400 recruitment offices of German firms in these countries, offering engagements that were thought to be of short-term nature.

Although these activities started already in the middle of the 1950s, they became more significant only after 1960.

Over time the nature of immigration changed considerably. At first, immigration was mostly labor migration. The migrant flows were in close correspondence with the German business cycle. Later on, this flexibility was reduced by the more permanent move of complete families to West Germany. Also, the flexibility of migrants from non-EC countries was hampered more by regulations than that of migrants from EC countries. In total, in the period from 1962 to 1973 gross immigration has been 9.66 million people and net immigration has been 3.68 million people, while the population grew to about 62 million people and unemployment rates kept to be low.

The *Consolidation Phase* (November 1973 - 1988) started in November 1973, when the labor recruitments were stopped abruptly in the face of increasing social tensions and the increasing fears about a recession after the first oil price shock. This phase is shown in the third panel of Table 2. Despite the halt of recruitments the desired drop in the foreign population could not be realized, since it turned out to be very difficult to convince migrants to leave the country. To the contrary, family members continued immigrating, and the foreign population was further increasing due to high fertility rates.

On November 25, 1981, a Federal law was established to induce a higher speed of return migration by giving financial incentives, by improving the information policy of the government, and by abolishing all kinds of bottlenecks hindering emigration. These measures were not very effective. Already in 1985, net immigration was again positive. Overall, the size of the foreign population in Germany increased by 22% from 1973 to 1989. 8.62 million people moved to West Germany from 1974 to 1988, and net immigration was 1.24 million people in this period.

In 1989, the political changes in the East induced the *German-German Migration Phase*, where, in total, gross immigration was 1.52 million people and net immigration was 0.98 million people, as shown in the fourth panel of Table 2. The most dominant feature of this phase is the massive flow per unit of time, as between twice and three times as many migrants came into West Germany as in an average year of the previous phase. The culmination of this development was around November 9, 1989, the day of the fall of the Berlin Wall, and, consequently, the breakdown of the inner German border. In 1990, the inflow of migrants reduced substantially after the announcement of the German Currency Union, which came into effect on July 1, 1990.

According to the German Federal Government and the Federal Board of Equalization, the "Bundesausgleichsamt", "Aussiedler" (repatriated persons) came mostly from Poland in 1989 (250,340 out of 377,055) and to a smaller part from the Soviet Union (98,134) and other East European states. In 1990, 397,073 "Aussiedler" came overall, 147,950 from the Soviet Union, 133,872 from Poland and 111,150 from Romania. 343,845 "Übersiedler" (East Germans migrating to West Germany) came in 1989 and 238,384 in 1990. The international nature of German-German migration from East Germany has been internalized by the German unification on October 3, 1990. Nevertheless, there is still substantial internal migration from the East of unified Germany to the West. This development is both natural and perhaps desirable in the face of the large economic differences between both parts of Germany.

4. Evaluation and Future Trends

This section evaluates the strength of past immigration in its relevance for the German economy and then demonstrates that the pressure exerted by this flow has been comparable to that experienced by the United States during the period of the largest relative inflow at the beginning of this century. Then these results are used to weigh Germany's prospective immigration experience. We expect the German economy to be able to successfully integrate a substantial migrant inflow.

The efficiency gains of immigration have to be contrasted with its cost. Social and cultural differences and differences in human capital generate a need for integration. On one hand there is potential social tension stemming from the fact that a measurable part of the population is "different". This social cost is associated with the stock of immigrants, and it should shrink as the immigrant population stays over time. On the other hand there are cost - social and economic - of integrating any entering migrant. They arise in various aspects of life, for example through necessary training at school or on the job, through increased work for administration, or through the need for housing allocation. These cost are associated with the migrant flow and we will concentrate on them in our discussion here. For Germany, the inflow of migrants, although substantial during all years, was varying in strength with the general economic conditions (see K.J.

Bade (1987)). This is most pronounced in the development of net immigration, which was even negative in 1967, from 1974 to 1976, and from 1982 to 1984.

We will argue here that gross immigration measures more precisely the burden that is imposed on an economy by migrant inflow than net immigration. For each entering migrant, most of the cost that we described above will arise, irrespective of the simultaneous outflow of emigrants. For instance, a firm experiences no reduction in training costs of a Turk if he replaces a Spanish worker. Integration cost will be lowest, if a worker enters the country repeatedly, but neither flow measure would be able to account for this.

To calculate a measure of the integration burden, it appears useful to normalize the migrant inflow by weighing it by the size of the population of the receiving country. Here we will weigh the average annual inflow of migrants into Germany for all four migration phases by the population size at the beginning of the phase. Using gross inflow in this calculation will lead to the calculation of gross relative inflow, using net inflow will lead to a measure of net relative inflow. These measures can then be interpreted as the average percentage of pre-period population that was entering the country every year within that phase.

Table 3 reports these numbers for the four distinct phases 1950 to 1961, 1962 to 1973, 1974 to 1988, and for 1989, and compares them to a measure calculated analogously for the United States in 1901 to 1910, a period when the largest inflow was observed there. On average, gross relative inflow was 1.09% in 1950 to 1961, the

Table 3:

Immigration to the Federal Republic of Germany (FRG) and the United States of America (USA)

	Relative Inflow[a] (%)	
	Gross	Net
USA		
1901 - 1910	1.16[b]	-
FRG		
1950 - 1961	1.09	0.61
1962 - 1973	1.42	0.54
1974 - 1988	0.93	0.13
1989	2.47	1.58
1991 - 2000[c]		
West Germany	0.57	-
United Germany	0.45	-

a Relative Inflow is average total inflow per year (gross or net) divided by beginning-of-the-period population size.

b Calculated from Statistical Abstracts of the United States, 1990, US Bureau of the Census, Washington, p. 7

c Scenario: All East European people of German origin move to Germany.

War Adjustment Phase, 1.42% in 1962 to 1973, the *Manpower Recruitment Phase*, 0.93% in 1974 to 1988, the *Consolidation Phase*, and 2.47% in 1989, the *German-German Migration Phase*. For the United States in 1901 to 1910 gross relative inflow was 1.16%.

This result argues for a direct comparability of the migration pressure to the United States and to Germany, even taking into account that a large part of migrants into Germany has been German speaking and perhaps required lower integration efforts. Clearly, the net relative inflow into Germany has been substantially smaller. Nevertheless, there are some strong indications that West Germany has been an immigration country ever since the end of World War II.

Was immigration beneficial for Germany? The fact that Germany has engaged in an active recruitment policy until 1973 suggests that West Germany has successfully managed its labor market problems by immigration. The relative strength of the pre-unification German economy despite the substantial integration cost exerted by migrant inflow also supports the belief that the German economy has generally benefitted from migration. This issue is not carefully investigated at the present time. Existing evidence only pertains to international data. Most of this international economic literature on the costs and benefits of migration into industrialized countries is evaluating the net effects as beneficial for the receiving country (see T. Straubhaar (1988); J.L. Simon (1989); G.J. Borjas (1990); and O. Stark (1991)).

Migrants into the United States are generally found to have higher labor force participation rates and higher saving rates, and are more often self-employed. This evidence is often interpreted as demonstrating that migrants are better motivated, more risk-taking and more innovative than natives. Regarding consequences for natives, empirical studies suggest that the (negative) labor market consequences of recent immigration are relatively small (see G.J. Borjas (1991) and K.F. Butcher and D. Card (1991)). First, one has to realize that immigrants tend to be of low educational level and therefore compete only with a small segment of the incumbent labor force for existing jobs. Second, the substitution elasticities of low-skill immigrant labor for low-skill native labor are relatively small and there are important supply side effects that create higher labor demand as a result of immigration.

Using these results, we now discuss in detail the immigration developments that Germany is likely to experience in future years. This development will be similar to that in other European countries, because despite the differences in Europe with respect to fertility, age structure, and other demographic components the major impact on migration will come from the change in East Europe. Barriers to the emigration of East Europeans have been removed and a large migration potential has been created by the economic adjustment process in the course of the economic reforms in the East European countries.

An initial incentive to migrate will come from the large differences in wage income and in the provision of public goods between West and East European countries. The main bulk of the migration potential, however, will stem from the enormous rise in unemployment that can be expected for the medium term period of adjustment. In the economic theory of migration, both income differences and unemployment are accepted as driving forces of migration, but preferences for the location of residence are taken to prevent migration if the differences in economic well-being at home and abroad are expected to be small.

Although there are several possible adjustment mechanisms that could help to prevent high unemployment in the Eastern labor markets, for instance the reduction of the high female labor force participation rates to the lower Western levels, and although it is unclear to which extent unemployment will occur if these adjustments fail to take place, it is already clear that the rise in unemployment will be severe enough to make migration profitable for millions of individuals.

The migration potential from the East will probably aim at the more prosperous neighboring countries with old links in the cultural and economic system: Germany, Austria and Italy. Germany will likely find most interest, albeit unified Germany is somewhat younger than West Germany. The OECD population prediction of 1988 had forecasted a substantial decline in the potential work force for West Germany (see OECD (1988)), measured by a drop of the size of the age group 15 to 64 from 42.3 million individuals (69.4% of the total population) in 1990 to a predicted 40.2 million people (67.9% of the total population) in 2000. This decline will now be more modest and the induced migration potential should shrink, too.

Still, there exist close cultural and historical ties with the East European countries, especially Hungary, Czechoslovakia, and Poland, and this will lead to a large migrant inflow. Mobility limitations will probably not be very effective in the long term, since it is not difficult to predict that these countries will be members of a larger European Community in the near future. Whereas previous experiences with de-regulations in the EC indicate that the de-regulation of intra-EC movements after 1992 will probably pose no substantial problem to the German economy, there might be a large additional migration potential realized through inflow from the South.

This will heavily depend on the integration policy of the EC with respect to Turkey, a country which has traditionally close links to Germany. The Turkish work potential measured as the size of the population aged 15 to 64 is predicted to rise from 34.9 million individuals in 1990 to 43.4 million people in 2000. This is a substantial increase and probably a large potential for migration into Germany.

A component of future German immigration whose magnitude is somewhat easier to predict is the potential of people of German origin currently residing in East Europe. This potential of "Aussiedler" (repatriated persons) can be derived from calculations by the German Ministry of Interior Affairs, which found that there are about 3.7 million people of German origin in East Europe. Of these, 1.9 million are currently living in the Soviet Union, 1 million in Poland, 0.4 million in Rumania, and 0.2 million in Hungary.

A scenario that evaluates the immigration pressure that could be exerted by this potential is shown in the last panel of Table 3. There we assumed that all these ethnic Germans move to Germany within the period from 1991 to 2000. Taking again the pre-period population size as a point of reference, the average relative inflow of migrants in this period would be 0.57% of the 1990 West German population per year, and 0.45% of the 1990 population of the united Germany per year.

In comparison to the relative gross inflow in other periods, for instance 1.42% in 1962 to 1973, these numbers do not indicate a dramatic development. Even if during this period about twice as many immigrants came, the immigration pressure would still be similar to that of the periods 1950 to 1961 or 1974 to 1988. In addition, the predicted drop in the size of the age group 15 to 64 for West Germany could be compensated by an inflow of young migrants from the East. A final evaluation would have to take into account, however, that if economic growth in former East Germany is lacking permanently, the increase in the labor force caused by unification might already more than outweigh the low West German fertility.

5. A European Perspective

What can we learn from the German experience? First, West Germany has been an immigration country ever since the end of World War II, and the inflow of migrants was highly correlated with a successful economic development. Without immigration, the German economy would have run into serious problems since the beginning of the 1960s due to labor shortage. During this process, the German economy was able to integrate a large number of immigrants, both in absolute and in relative terms. Apart from the last immigration phase in 1989, Germany's ability to integrate this large amount of migrants was supported by the fact that the stream was relatively evenly spread out over time.

Second, Germany's experience shows that it seems easier to induce immigration than to control or reduce the size of the migrant flow once the initial impact for immigration has been given. At least until the 1970s, immigration was following the needs of the labor market and was not out of control of policy makers. Since then, the situation was more difficult to monitor. Even when strong measures of immigration regulation are existent, it is difficult to regulate the immigration of family members of immigrants already in residence. Furthermore, an economy with a generous unemployment insurance and welfare system will not easily be able to induce return migration. All German policy measures aiming at an increase of return migration were not very successful, and there is similar experience in other European countries (see M. Frey (1986) and H. Körner (1986)).

What can we infer for the future immigration experience of other European countries? As indicated, it is speculated that between 5 and 40 million people could move from the East to the West. Abstracting from other migration potentials in the South of Europe, in North Africa, and in other parts of the less developed world, we will try to evaluate how dramatic the situation really is. We have seen that Germany will be the country most likely to receive the bulk of the East-West migration. However, all other European countries, especially those in the EC, will have to expect some immigration pressure.

At least partly, increasing immigration to these countries will merely outweigh the excess demand on the labor markets that threatens to be a consequence of low and below-replacement fertility rates in many European countries. The European population will stagnate within the next 10 to 20 years if not corrected by immigration. This is significantly different from the post World War II situation, where a large increase in population size in the key countries France, West Germany, Italy, The Netherlands, and the United Kingdom of about 33.5 million people was observed.

In fact, there were debates in France and Germany whether the rapid fertility decline would cause economic problems. At the moment, this discussion has been pushed in the background by what is felt to be the large immigration problem. This view overlooks that immigration would help to compensate for population losses and to stabilize the economic system as long as the necessary market adjustments and structural changes take place. From the German example, one can learn that European economies seem to be able to integrate large flows of entering migrants. Rather than a problem of the ultimate magnitude of the flows, it appears that the rate of entry is the key issue.

The potential economic benefits of immigration have thereby be weighed against their cost. Some of the immigrants will be unemployed and thus a burden to the welfare state, others will crowd out natives. In addition, there are social and cultural aspects. A multi-cultural society has to find acceptance in the native population. Thus, although migration flows might generally be useful to smooth out interregional or national differences and to realize efficiency gains, integration cost might rise with the magnitude of the migration stream and limit the size of the optimal inflow of migrants.

Even abstracting from any cost, long-term perspectives might prevent large migration streams from being desirable for both emigration and immigration countries. Since Germany's example has shown that individual migration decisions do not seem to be easily reversible and appear to have repercussions for the migration decisions of family members, an emigration country might loose long-term growth potential through migrant outflow, even if it alleviates unemployment in the short term. An immigration country, on the other hand, should realize that immigrants tend to stay, even if the original disequilibrium situation on the labor market that initiated their recruitment from abroad has passed or has even been reversed. Therefore, it should seek for immigration on a reasonable scale.

These arguments suggest that the affected countries on both the sending and the receiving sides of migration could profitably engage in a common policy to control the ensuing migration stream. What scale is ultimately deemed reasonable is yet open to debate. Without more experience, perhaps through the observation of the performance of a small and controlled immigrant flow over some future years, its benefits and costs are hard to predict. It seems generally sensible, though, to tailor the stream in accordance with the needs of the receiving labor market.

Another key determinant of the success of such an immigration policy will be the correct choice of citizenship regulations. In the moment, the economic migration literature offers arguments for both the promotion of temporary over permanent and of permanent over temporary migration (see O. Stark (1991)). The first strategy would be supported if the economic performance of migrants turned out to be higher the higher the probability of return migration, and vice versa. More work has to be done on the empirical level to clarify these issues.

References:

Bade, K.J. (1987), Transatlantic Emigration and Continental Immigration: the German Experience Past and Present, in K.J. Bade (ed.), **Population, Labour and Migration in 19th- and 20th-Century Germany**. Leamington Spa et al., Berg Publishers Lim.

Borjas, G.J. (1990), **Friends or Strangers: The Impact of Immigrants on the U.S. Economy**. New York, Basic Books.

Borjas, G.J. (1991), Immigrants in the U.S. Labor Market, in: **American Economic Review**, 81, 287-291.

Butcher, K.F. and D. Card (1991), Immigration and Wages: Evidence from the 1980's, in: **American Economic Review**, 81, 292-296.

Frey, M. (1986), Direkte und indirekte Rückkehrförderung seitens der Aufnahmeländer. Überblick, in: H. Körner and U. Mehrländer (eds.), **Die "neue" Ausländerpolitik in Europa. Erfahrungen in den Aufnahme- und Entsendeländern**. Bonn, Verlag Neue Gesellschaft, 15-63.

Körner, H. (1986), Das Gesetz zur Förderung der Rückkehrbereitschaft von Ausländern vom 28. November 1983 - Eine kritische Bilanz, in: H. Körner and U. Mehrländer (eds.), **Die "neue" Ausländerpolitik in Europa. Erfahrungen in den Aufnahme- und Entsendeländern**. Bonn, Verlag Neue Gesellschaft, 65-72.

OECD (1988), **Ageing Populations: The Social Policy Implications**. Paris.

Stark, O. (1991), **The Migration of Labor**. Cambridge, Basil Blackwell.

Straubhaar, T. (1988), **On the Economics of International Labor Migration**. Bern, Haupt Verlag.

The Economic Consequences of Selective Immigration Policies*

Jozef M.M. Ritzen

Hendrik P. van Dalen

Abstract: The divergence in demographic development between Europe and many other parts of the world is likely to lead to selective immigration of well-trained labor from developing countries into Western Europe.

The policy of a selective immigration policy is studied here with a two-country economic growth model. The welfare effects are considered for both the country of emigration and of immigration. This policy is compared to the situation where countries abstain from selective immigration policies.

An immigration policy is likely to be restricted to skilled labor. A constant migration flow from the country with a high population growth rate to the country with a lower growth rate is shown to be generally a Pareto-inferior policy. To obtain optimal growth, an investment policy in human and physical capital is the preferable alternative.

---

* The authors gratefully acknowledge comments by Walt McMahon. An earlier version was presented at the Second Annual meeting of the European Society for Population Economics at the University of Mannheim, June 1988.

1. Introduction

The future development of the population in Western Europe is likely to lead to shortages of well-trained young adults in the next decade. Three possible policy alternatives are presently discussed in the light of limiting such shortages and their effects on the economy. One alternative is to raise the educational level of the working population as a whole by increased training and retraining efforts. The second alternative is to institute immigration policies which allow well-trained youngsters to immigrate in Western Europe. The third option is to increase the labor force participation rate of young well-trained women.

In this paper we shall first (in section 2) describe why we expect shortages of well-trained youngsters on the labor market(s) in Western Europe by the year 2000. The three policy alternatives are also explored in that section. Section 3 presents an analytical framework to evaluate the effects of two of these policies, i.e. training versus immigration or draining. The framework is a two-country growth model. Only singular solutions are considered to be relevant for further scrutiny. The third policy alternative is not further analyzed here. Section 4 presents a simulation study of the consequences of a constant migration flow. Section 5 summarizes the findings.

2. Policy Options for the Labor Market in an Ageing Society

In Western Europe birth rates have substantially dropped in the period 1964-1970 after a period of a baby boom starting around 1945. Since the average life expectancy at birth has continued to increase (although only slightly) Western Europe is to be an ageing continent until the mid-half of the next century. If birth rates and life expectancy would from now on remain fairly constant, the fraction of the elderly in the population is likely to increase substantially until about 2050. Not only would the fraction of the young decrease in the years to come, but this group would also decrease in absolute size. The supply of young workers will decrease even faster, since the participation in education continues to increase, if only to a minor extent. Some compensation in this development can be found in the tendency to increased labor market participation of young women. It is, however, unclear to what extent saturation in this development has already taken place on a level of about 60% for the age group 20-30 years. In any case, even if present trends were extrapolated, the increase in the female labor market participation rate cannot fully offset the decrease in the labor supply of persons between 20 and 30 years of age. For the Netherlands, for instance, this group will decline by 25% between 1990 and the year 2005 (CPB (1983)). To be sure: if this development would lead to shortages on the labor market, and if as a consequence wages would rise then an additional female worker effect could be induced, since female labor market participation tends to be wage elastic. This has not been taken into account in the extrapolations. On the whole, however, we conclude that a decline in the supply of young persons is likely.

On the demand side well-trained youngsters can be viewed as a separate production factor. In the absence of substantial retraining efforts for older workers, young workers are the only ones to embody the latest knowledge and are thus an important factor for technical progress. Support for the hypothesis of an important role of well-trained youngsters for technical progress can be found in Ritzen (1985, p.160). Almost 40% of "autonomous" technical progress could for time series data of the Netherlands for the period 1960-1980 be explained by the proportion of young university graduates within the working population. If these assumptions are correct then the substitutability between young well-trained workers and other factors of production is, in the absence of retraining, limited as well. Also it is then likely that the demand for this group of workers will continue to increase. In the absence of a sufficiently large supply, the human capital structure could be sub-optimal in sense of Prescott and Boyd (1987). If workers' productivity not only depends on individual human capital, but also on the human capital of colleagues within the organization, an externality may arise which, in the circumstances of an ageing society, might well be negative.

Combining considerations of supply and demand, we conclude that a shortage of well-trained young workers is likely to emerge in Western Europe. The present debates on how to counter the ill effects due to this shortage are thus well founded.

One of the alternatives put forward in those debates is to increase *retraining efforts of "older" workers* (above the age of 30). As shown by van Imhoff (1989) it becomes more attractive for a nation to invest in education when the population growth rate falls. Thus the optimal training effort should move in the opposite direction of the growth rate of population. At present retraining is quite limited in Western Europe (see Schütze and Instance (1988)). A survey shows for the Netherlands that in 1987 no more than 1.5%

of all wage costs are devoted to retraining. This includes the opportunity, the direct and the indirect, overhead costs of training departments of industries (CBS, 1988), while according to international comparisons, the Netherlands is a "leader" in terms of retraining efforts. Substantial barriers seem to prohibit that retraining on large scale will emerge. First of all, the costs of training, and in particular, the opportunity costs, of older workers are high. Second, external effects, inherent in retraining, impair an optimal supply by market forces. Third, at present there is considerable pressure on government funds, which makes it difficult for government to stimulate retraining by subsidization. This pressure is due to existing budget deficits and the wide-spread desire to cut taxes. Third, the time delay between the investment in retraining and its return is substantial. This is not conducive to action on this issue by politicians who feel constrained by political business cycles of four years. Fourth, collective bargaining leaves too small a margin for a reasonably speedy establishment of substantial retraining efforts.

The second policy alternative aimed at avoiding a shortage of well-trained young workers is the institution of a *selective immigration policy*. In Canada, Foot (1986) has argued in favor of such a policy, while in the U.S. such a policy has already been in practice for the last decade. A selective immigration policy obviously conforms to the behavior of politicians which look for short-run results. Economic history (see Foreman-Peck (1983, p.154)) has shown that sending countries, such as European countries at the end of the nineteenth century, bore the cost of supporting and training citizens from infancy, but reaped little benefit when they reached the working age. Conversely, receiving countries, such as the U.S.A., Australia and Argentina, obtained the benefits without bearing the costs, thus acting as a free rider.

A selective immigration policy is only a feasible alternative as long as there is a supply of potential immigrants. The factors determining such a supply have been widely discussed and empirically established in the literature[1]. A sufficient condition for a considerable supply of potential immigrants is a large disparity in the wages of potential immigrants in the country of immigration and of origin. Such a disparity exists at the moment between Europe and many developing countries. There are no indications that this wage gap will be lessened in the next decade.

One should however consider the disadvantages of a selective immigration policy. For the country of immigration there are two clear disadvantages. First also selective immigration policies often turn out to be less selective than they show at first sight. Allowances for family reunion in the present laws will make the age distribution of the immigrants plus their dependents much less peaked. Second there are adaptation costs of immigrants. For the country of origin, the disadvantages are more substantial. The assets in human capital have been built up mainly with general funds. Now part of them vanishes. Bhagwati (e.g. 1978) has repeatedly pointed out that a brain drain is a disequalizing force in a world with already high income disparities between the countries of immigration and the countries of emigration.

1 See e.g. Sjaastad (1960), Wilkinson (1970), Greenwood (1985) and Heijke (1987). For an excellent collection of articles on the issue of the brain drain one is referred to Bhagwati (1976) and Bhagwati and Partington (1976).

An important point which until now has often been ignored is that migration flows affect capital flows. Immigration is not only a substitute for human capital investments in the country of immigration but it can also be a substitute for foreign investment by that country, particularly in a world of diverging populations. This aspect has further been elaborated in the following section.

One aspect which is not entirely clear is whether immigration gives rise to a potential Pareto improvement. If this were the case then the countries of immigration could reimburse the countries of origin and both would gain.

The third policy alternative, *raising the participation rate of well-trained young women*, is not considered further in the scope of this paper.

3. Migration as a Policy Alternative

Presently we will analyze the welfare consequences of an immigration policy with the help of an optimal international growth model. The formulation of the two-country model is an extension of the model of van Dalen and Ritzen (1988) by including training and migration. The analysis focusses on intercountry migration between two countries with a constant population growth. It is thus more general than the preceding comments in section 2. It is possible, however, to extend the model in order to account for non-stationarities in population growth. Earlier studies on the implications of migration on the welfare of the country of immigration or emigration were done by Rodriguez, (1975, 1976), Brecher and Choudhri (1987) and Tu (1988). In Rodriguez's model, numerous constraints are imposed on the interaction between the country of immigration and emigration, like the absence of capital flows between the countries. In this study the latter restriction is removed. Brecher and Choudhri *do* introduce capital mobility, but their model starts from the assumption of identical technologies, fixed factor endowments and rigid real wages. They show that the optimal degree of labor migration is zero and that national welfare can always be maximized by an optimal capital flow. Tu's analysis is also of a static nature. He tries to establish the welfare consequences of international migration on the basis of generally accepted assumptions. He concludes that the receiving country cannot lose from immigration in the forms of higher per capita income if the extra output produced but not claimed by immigrants is divided among the original population. The sending country enjoys higher income per capita as a result of emigration. The world as a whole benefits from international migration in his model.

One of the complications of analyzing migration as a continuous process through time is the way in which it affects the transition and steady state behavior of the economy (as noted by Bhagwati and Rodriguez (1976, p.100). This section will not look into the question of the transition path; it concentrates on the steady state of the economies.

The maximization problem is the same as in the earlier study (van Dalen and Ritzen (1988)): the planning board of each of the countries decides on the key economic control variables such that the discounted flow of consumption in the own country is maximized. The entire future control path of the other country is taken as given. The equilibria we calculate are thus Nash equilibria.

The key economic control variables in the model are investments in physical and human capital. Government is considered not to have control over emigration, i.e. it can not stop people who wish to leave the country. However, it can control the flow of (permanent) *im*migrants. The potential differential creates a migration force.

The general formulation of the two-country model is omitted here. We refer to van Dalen and Ritzen (1988) for that purpose. We concentrate on the situation where country 1 is the industrialized country with a low rate of population growth and country 2 is the developing country with a higher rate of population growth. For simplicity's sake we shall call country 1 the "rich" and country 2 the "poor" country. In van Dalen and Ritzen (1988) we showed that, in general, for these population growth rates, only the rich country invests in the poor country and not vice versa. This we take to be a first point of departure. A second point of departure is that the wage rates in the rich country exceed those of the poor country. Actual migration is then determined by the admission of immigrants in the rich country. This country maximizes its discounted flow of per capita future consumption by means of the following control variables:

$s_{11}(t)$ Investments in the own country (1) as a fraction of Gross National Product (GNP) at time t.

$s_{12}(t)$ Investments by the rich country in the poor country as a fraction of GNP of the rich country at time t.

$u_1(t)$ Investments in training in the rich country as a fraction ot its GNP at time t.

$d_o(t)$ The number of immigrants with education level 0 (i.e. low level) admitted at time t in the rich country as a fraction of its total population.

$d_1(t)$ The number of immigrants with educational level I (i.e. high level) admitted at time t in the rich country as a fraction of its total population.

The control variables exceed the state variables; the system is overdetermined. We shall therefore focus either on optimal training when a selective immigration policy is given or on optimal immigration when the training policy has been predetermined.

Population of the rich country grows as a result of new born children, (minus) mortality and immigration:

$$\dot{L}_1/L_1 = n_1 + d_o(t) + d_1(t) = m_1(t) \quad (1)$$

where n_1 is an exogenous fixed rate of natural increase and m_1 the aggregate population growth rate.

Per capita physical capital then develops as follows (omitting the time variables for notational convenience):

$$\dot{k}_{11} = s_{11}g_1 - (\delta_k + m_1)k_{11} \quad (2)$$

$$\dot{k}_{12} = s_{12}g_1 - (\delta_k + m_1)k_{12} \quad (3)$$

where k_{ij} (for j = 1,2) represents the physical capital stock owned by country 1 in country *j*, δ_k the depreciation rate of physical capital and g_1 is the gross national product of the rich country:

$$g_1 = f(k_{11}, h_{10}, h_{11}) + r_2 k_{12} \tag{4}$$

Here r_2 is the interest rate in the poor country.

The production function $f(\cdot)$ is homogeneous of degree 1 in terms of physical capital (k_{11}) and the two types of human capital: untrained or "raw" labor (as a fraction of the population: h_{10}) and trained labor h_{11}. Following Ritzen (1977, ch. 3) human capital is accumulated through an educational process which involves training costs in country one of η_1, to be associated with the training of a unit of labor from level 0 to level 1, and the formation of human capital uses up part (u_1) of the national product:

$$\dot{h}_{11} = u_1 g_1 / \eta_1 - (\delta_H + m_1) h_{11} + d_1 \tag{5}$$

The constraints on the state variables are:

$$h_{10} + h_{11} = 1 \tag{6}$$

$$k_{11}, k_{12} \geq 0 \tag{7}$$

$$0 \leq h_{10}, h_{11} \leq 1 \tag{8}$$

and on the control variables:

$$0 \leq u_1 + s_{11} + s_{12} \leq 1 \tag{9}$$

$$0 \le d_0 \le h_{20} \tag{10}$$

$$0 \le d_1 \le h_{21} \tag{11}$$

Per capita consumption amounts to the following expression:

$$c_1 = (1 - s_{11} - s_{12} - u_1)\, g_1 - p_0 d_0 - p_1 d_1 \tag{12}$$

where p_0 and p_1 represent the adaptation costs per unit of immigrant labor. These adaptation costs also include a tax on the use of foreign labor to be levied by the country of origin. Since taxes do not as yet exist we shall ignore them in the model. The costs p_0 and p_1 reduce consumption in the rich country without increasing consumption in the poor country.

The maximization of the flow of consumption discounted by a social rate of time preference ρ_1 is achieved if the Hamiltonian is maximized at each point in time, the Euler-Lagrange equations are satisfied as well as the transversality conditions.

The Hamiltonian is:

$$\begin{aligned} H = {} & e^{-\rho 1t} c_1 + \lambda_{11}\left(s_{11} g_1 - (\delta_k + m_1)k_{11}\right) + \\ & + \lambda_{12}\left(s_{12} g_1 - (\delta_k + m_1)k_{12}\right) + \\ & + \lambda_{13}\left(u_1 g_1/\eta_1 - (\delta_H + m_1)h_{11} + d_1\right) \end{aligned} \tag{13}$$

The Euler-Lagrange equations are the three state equations and the following three costate equations:

$$\dot{\lambda}_{11} = -\frac{\partial H}{\partial k_{11}} = \lambda_{11}(\delta_K + m_1) - s_{11}g'_{11}(\lambda_{11} - e^{-\rho 1t}) -$$

$$- s_{12}g'_{11}(\lambda_{12} - e^{-\rho 1t}) - u_1 g'_{11}(\lambda_{13}/\eta_1 - e^{-\rho 1t}) -$$

$$- e^{-\rho 1t}g'_{11} \tag{14}$$

$$\dot{\lambda}_{12} = -\frac{\partial H}{\partial k_{12}} = \lambda_{12}(\delta_K + m_1) - s_{11}g'_{12}(\lambda_{11} - e^{-\rho 1t}) -$$

$$- s_{12}g'_{12}(\lambda_{12} - e^{-\rho 1t}) - u_1 g'_{12}(\lambda_{13}/\eta_1 - e^{-\rho 1t}) -$$

$$- e^{-\rho 1t}g'_{12} \tag{15}$$

where $g'_{ij} = -\frac{\partial H}{\partial h_{11}} = \lambda_{13}(\partial_H + m_1) - s_{11}\Delta w_1(\lambda_{11} - e^{-\rho 1t}) -$

$$- s_{12}\Delta w_1(\lambda_{12} - e^{-\rho 1t}) - u_1\Delta w_1(\lambda_{13}/\eta_1 - e^{-\rho 1t}) -$$

$$- e^{-\rho 1t}\Delta w_1 \tag{16}$$

where $\Delta w_1 = w_{11} - w_{10} = \partial f_1/\partial h_{11} - \partial f_1/\partial h_{10}$.

We are only interested in steady state paths and hence search for singular solutions of this problem. The road towards this singular solution from some initial condition or away from this solution towards some terminal time condition is beyond the perspective of this paper.

Singular solutions are likely to emerge as the Hamiltonian is linear in the control variables:

$$H = s_{11}g_1(\lambda_{11} - e^{-\rho 1t}) + s_{12}g_1(\lambda_{12} - e^{-\rho 1t}) +$$
$$+ u_1 g_1(\lambda_{13}/\eta_1 - e^{-\rho 1t}) +$$
$$+ d_o(-\lambda_{11}k_{11} - \lambda_{12}k_{12} - \lambda_{13}h_{11} - p_o e^{-\rho 1t}) +$$
$$+ d_1(-\lambda_{11}k_{11} - \lambda_{12}k_{12} - \lambda_{13}(h_{11} - 1) - p_1 e^{-\rho 1t}) +$$
$$+ \text{terms in which the control variables do not appear.} \quad (17)$$

A. Let us first consider the case when immigration is exogenous. The optimal steady state is achieved on singular solutions for:

$$\lambda_{11} = \lambda_{12} = e^{-\rho 1t} \text{ and } \lambda_{13} = \eta_1 e^{-\rho 1t} \quad (18)$$

so that the Golden Rule of Capital Accumulation is characterized by the extension of Ritzen (1977) and van Dalen and Ritzen (1988). For physical capital the investment rules are:

$$\frac{\partial f_1}{\partial k_{11}} = m_1 + \delta_K + \rho_1 \quad (19)$$

$$\frac{\partial f_2}{\partial k_2} + k_{12} \frac{\partial^2 f_2}{\partial k_2} \Theta^{-1} = m_1 + \partial_K + \rho_1 \quad (20)$$

The term $f_2(\cdot)$ represents the production function of the poor country, k_2 total investments in country 2 (i.e. $k_2 = k_{22} + k_{12}\Theta^{-1}$) and Θ denotes the population ratio between the poor and the rich country:

$$\Theta(t) = L_2(t)/L_1(t) \tag{21}$$

The Golden Rule for human capital amounts to keeping the difference in wage rates equal to the training costs, taking into account impatience, population growth and obsolescence of human capital.

$$\Delta w_1 = \eta_1(m_1 + \delta_H + \rho_1) \tag{22}$$

B. Subsequently we consider the case when human capital accumulation and the immigration of skilled labor is exogenous. The switching function for d_o in the Hamiltonian is only non-negative if the shadow price of trained labor (λ_{13}) is negative, i.e. if an overaccumulation of human capital has occured. The singular solutions for this case are determined by

$$\lambda_{11} = \lambda_{12} = e^{-\rho 1t} \text{ and}$$

$$\lambda_{13}h_{11} = -\lambda_{11}k_{11} - \lambda_{12}k_{12} - p_o e^{-\rho 1t} \tag{23}$$

Combining the first with the second part yields:

$$\lambda_{13} = -(k_{11} + k_{12} + p_o)e^{-\rho 1t}/h_{11} \tag{24}$$

Substitution in the co-state equations yields the following three golden rules:

$$\pi(\partial f_1/\partial k_{11}) = m_1 + \delta_K + \rho_1 \tag{25}$$

with $\pi = \left(1 - u_1(k_{11} + k_{12} + p_O + h_{11}\eta)/\eta_1 h_{11}\right)$. This rule says that the larger u_1 is, the smaller is π and the larger k_{11} should be.

$$\left\{\frac{\partial f_2}{\partial k_2} + k_{12}\,\frac{\partial^2 f_2}{\partial k_2^2}\,\Theta^{-1}\right\}\pi = m_1 + \delta_K + \rho_1 \tag{26}$$

$$\Delta w_1 \pi = -\left((k_{11} + k_{12} + p_O)/h_{11}\right)(m_1 + \delta_H + \rho_1) + $$

$$-\left\{\frac{\dot{k}_{11} + \dot{k}_{12}}{h_{11}} - \frac{\dot{h}_{11}(k_{11} + k_{12} + p_O)}{h_{11}^2}\right\} \tag{27}$$

C. Finally, we focus on the case with trained immigration as the policy variable. This case is analogous to the second case (B). The singular solution for this case is determined by

$$\lambda_{11} = \lambda_{12} = e^{-\rho 1t} \tag{28}$$

and

$$\lambda_{13}(1 - h_{11}) = \lambda_{11}k_{11} + \lambda_{12}k_{12} + p_1 e \tag{29}$$

Substitution in the co-state equations yields now the golden rules:

$$\psi(\partial f_1/\partial k_{11}) = m_1 + \delta_K + \rho_1 \tag{30}$$

$$\text{where } \psi = \left\{1 + u_1\left[\frac{k_{11} + k_{12} + p_1 - \eta_1(1 - h_{11})}{\eta_1(1 - h_{11})}\right]\right\}$$

$$\left\{\frac{\partial f_2}{\partial k_2} + k_{12}\frac{\partial^2 f_2}{\partial k_2^2}\Theta^{-1}\right\} = m_1 + \delta_k + p_1 \tag{31}$$

$$\Delta w_1\psi = \left((k_{11} + k_{12} + p_1)/(1 - h_{11})\right)(m_1 + \delta_H + \rho_1) +$$

$$-\left\{\frac{\dot{k}_{11} + \dot{k}_{12}}{1 - h_{11}} + \frac{\dot{h}_{11}(k_{11} + k_{12} + p_1)}{(1 - h_{11})^2}\right\} \tag{32}$$

For all three cases the Nash-equilibrium implies that the golden rules for the poor country are given by

$$\frac{\partial f_2}{\partial k_2} - k_{12}\frac{\partial^2 f_2}{\partial k_2^2}\Theta^{-1} = n_2 + \rho_2 + \delta_K - (d_o + d_1)\Theta^{-1} \tag{33}$$

and

$$\Delta w_2 = \eta_2(n_2 + (d_o + d_1)\Theta^{-1} + \delta_H + \rho_2) \tag{34}$$

Rule (20) in combination with rule (33) yields:

$$\frac{\partial f_2}{\partial k_2} = \delta_K + \frac{1}{2}(n_2 + \rho_2 + n_1 + \rho_1) + \frac{1}{2}(d_o + d_1)(1 - \Theta^{-1}) \tag{35}$$

Because of the complexities of the cases B and C we focus on case A and compose different *constant* immigration policies. For this subcase it is clear from equations (19) and (22) that k_{11}, h_{11} and h_{10} are constant. Differentiation with respect to time of rules (34) and (35) yields:

$$\begin{pmatrix} \beta_{11} & (\beta_{12} - \beta_{13}) \\ \beta_{12} - \beta_{13}) & (\beta_{22} + \beta_{33} - 2\beta_{23}) \end{pmatrix} \begin{pmatrix} \dot{k}_2 \\ \dot{h}_{21} \end{pmatrix} =$$

$$= (d_o + d_1)\Theta^{-2}\dot{\Theta} \begin{pmatrix} 1/2 \\ \eta_2 \end{pmatrix} \qquad (36)$$

where $\beta_{ij} = \partial^2 f_2/\partial q_i \partial q_j$ for i, j = 1,2,3 and $q_1 = k_2$, $q_2 = h_{21}$ and $q_3 = h_{20}$, with

$$\dot{\Theta} = \Theta(n_2 - m_1) - (d_o + d_1) \qquad (37)$$

For constant immigration this means that

$$\Theta = \Big(d_o + d_1 + (\Theta_o(n_2 - m_1) -$$

$$- (d_o + d_1))e^{(n2-m1)t}\Big)\Big/(n_2 - m_1) \qquad (38)$$

Note that $d\Theta/dt > 0$ in order to remain within the assumptions of the model. The determinant (D) of the matrix is:

$$D = \beta_{11}(\beta_{22} + \beta_{33} - 2\beta_{23}) - (\beta_{12} - \beta_{13})^2 \tag{39}$$

The development of capital in country 2 is then determined by:

$$\begin{pmatrix} \dot{k}_2 \\ \\ \dot{h}_{21} \end{pmatrix} = (d_o + d_1)\ \Theta^{-2}\dot{\Theta}\ /$$

$$/\ D \begin{pmatrix} (\beta_{22} + \beta_{33} - 2\beta_{23}) & -(\beta_{12} - \beta_{13}) \\ \\ -(\beta_{12} - \beta_{13}) & \beta_{11} \end{pmatrix} \begin{pmatrix} 1/2 \\ \\ \eta_2 \end{pmatrix}$$

or

$$k = (d_o + d_1)\ \Theta^{-2}\Theta\ /\ D\ \Big({}^1\!/_2\, \beta_{22} + {}^1\!/_2 \beta_{33} - \beta_{23} - \eta_2(\beta_{12} - \beta_{13})\Big) \tag{40}$$

$$\dot{h} = (d_o + d_1)\Theta^{-2}\Theta/D\ \Big(-{}^1\!/_2(\beta_{12} - \beta_{13}) + \eta_2\beta_{11}\Big) \tag{41}$$

Note that the country 2 reacts identically to emigration of trained labor and untrained labor over time.

Capital accumulation in the poor country by the poor country is:

$$\dot{k}_{22} = \dot{k}_2 + \Theta^{-2}k_{12}\dot{\Theta} - \Theta^{-1}\dot{k}_{12} \tag{42}$$

When immigration is absent it follows that k_2, h_{21} and h_{20} are constant. However, immigration will lead to non-constant per capita capital in country two. In many cases the determinant D will be positive and $\beta_{12} > \beta_{13}$. In those cases total physical and human capital in country 2 will decline over time.

4. A Simulation Study of a Constant Migration Flow

Here we illustrate the theoretical findings of the previous section, with particular attention to the welfare consequences of a constant migration flow, while human capital is accumulated optimally.

The production technologies of both countries are assumed to be of a Cobb-Douglas nature[2]. The countries differ in their production technology. Tables 1 and 2 summarize the main findings for two sets of coefficients. These differ not only in the training costs but also in the constants of the Cobb-Douglas production function. In Table 1 we present the results for the case where the training costs in the rich country are much higher than in the poor country. The constants of the production function are relatively high (compared to case 2), so that training costs are relatively low. This case we call low and differing training costs.

In Table 2 the results are presented for the case where the training costs are the same for the poor and for the rich country. Now the constants of the production function are relatively low. This is the case of high and identical training costs.

2 With homogenous physical capital and heterogenous human capital the model had to be solved by an iteration procedure, for which we used a Newton-Raphson algorithm.

Table 1:

Illustration of Optimal Economic Growth with and without Migration: low and differing training costs

	$d_1 = 0$			$d_1 = 0.001$		
t =	0	30	50	0	30	50
k_{11}	157.57	157.57	157.57	149.99	149.99	149.99
k_{12}	50.67	112.78	374.43	40.54	81.52	236.55
k_{22}	131.75	131.75	131.75	141.89	137.92	135.25
h_{11}	0.459	0.459	0.459	0.457	0.457	0.457
h_{21}	0.309	0.309	0.309	0.309	0.309	0.309
s_{11}	0.093	0.085	0.064	0.098	0.092	0.076
s_{12}	0.054	0.111	0.275	0.044	0.083	0.200
s_{22}	0.244	0.244	0.244	0.239	0.243	0.244
u_1	0.038	0.035	0.026	0.037	0.035	0.029
u_2	0.018	0.018	0.018	0.018	0.018	0.018
c_1	69.18	70.99	78.63	68.10	69.39	74.25
c_2	35.92	35.92	35.92	37.01	36.47	36.10
W	105.10	150.94	344.08	105.11	151.69	332.66

Table 1: continued

	$d_1 = 0$			$d_1 = 0.001$		
t =	0	30	50	0	30	50
$\Sigma\ c_1$	69.18	930.48	1,339.07	68.10	913.78	1,308.98
$\Sigma\ c_2$	35.92	478.84	679.09	37.01	489.98	692.25
ΣW	105.10	1,614.37	2,781.48	105.11	1,612.82	2,773.46

The following parameters are used for this simulation:

$A_1 = 50$ $\quad A_2 = 10$

$\alpha_1 = 0.2$ $\quad \alpha_2 = 0.4$

$\beta_1 = 0.4$ $\quad \beta_2 = 0.2$

where α_i and β_i denote the Cobb-Douglas production coefficients of the form

$$y_i = A_i k_i^{\alpha} h_{i1}^{\beta} h_{i0}^{\gamma}, \gamma = 1 - \alpha - \beta \text{ (for } i = 1,2)$$

$n_1 = 0$ $\quad n_2 = 0.04$

$\rho_1 = 0.05$ $\quad \rho_2 = 0.05$

$\eta_1 = 70$ $\quad \eta_2 = 20$

$P_1 = 0$ $\quad \delta_K = 0.05$

$L_1(0)=L_2(0)=1$ $\quad \delta_H = 0.10$

and W denotes the weighted sum of consumption $L_1c_1 + L_2c_2$, whereas the Σ-sign denotes the summation over time taking into account time preference.

Table 2:

Illustration of Optimal Economic Growth with and without Migration: high and identical training costs

	$d_1 = 0$			$d_1 = 0.001$		
t =	0	30	50	0	30	50
k_{11}	9.72	9.72	9.72	9.56	9.56	9.56
k_{12}	0.37	0.83	2.76	0.36	0.77	2.47
k_{22}	0.97	0.97	0.97	0.99	0.98	0.98
h_{11}	0.152	0.152	0.152	0.150	0.150	0.150
h_{21}	0.006	0.006	0.006	0.006	0.006	0.006
s_{11}	0.099	0.098	0.094	0.100	0.099	0.095
s_{12}	0.007	0.015	0.048	0.007	0.014	0.044
s_{22}	0.244	0.244	0.244	0.242	0.243	0.244
u_1	0.217	0.214	0.205	0.204	0.202	0.194
u_2	0.164	0.164	0.164	0.355	0.253	0.191
c_1	3.32	3.34	3.39	3.36	3.37	3.42
c_2	0.21	0.21	0.21	0.15	0.18	0.20
W	3.53	3.81	4.96	3.50	3.84	5.06

Table 2: continued

	$d_1 = 0$			$d_1 = 0.001$		
t =	0	30	50	0	30	50
$\Sigma\, c_1$	3.32	44.34	63.03	3.36	44.81	63.68
$\Sigma\, c_2$	0.21	2.83	4.02	0.15	2.17	3.24
$\Sigma\, W$	3.53	48.39	71.57	3.50	47.95	70.92

The following parameters are used for this simulation:

$A = 7$ $\quad A_2 = 1$

$\alpha_1 = 0.2$ $\quad \alpha_2 = 0.4$

$\beta_1 = 0.4$ $\quad \beta_2 = 0.2$

where α_i and β_i denote the Cobb-Douglas production coefficients of the form

$y_i = A_i k_i^{\alpha} h_{i1}^{\beta} h_{i0}^{\gamma}$, $\gamma = 1 - \alpha - \beta$ (for $i = 1,2$)

$n_1 = 0$ $\quad n_2 = 0.04$

$\rho_1 = 0.05$ $\quad \rho_2 = 0.05$

$\eta_1 = 70$ $\quad \eta_2 = 70$

$P_1 = 0$ $\quad \delta_K = 0.05$

$L_1(0) = L_2(0) = 1$ $\quad \delta_H = 0.10$

and W denotes the weighted sum of consumption $L_1c_1 + L_2c_2$, whereas the Σ-sign denotes the summation over time taking into account time preference.

A general observation is that the welfare gains and losses of migration depend heavily on the production technologies in use and on the training costs. The following intermediate conclusions can be drawn from the comparison of optimal economic growth paths with and without migration:

1. Migration is a substitute for international borrowing and lending. The capital stock k_{12} falls steeply compared to the case of no migration. This observation has far-reaching consequences.

2. When labor mobility is *excluded*, the rich country (with the low rate of population growth) will constantly increase its capital holdings in the poor country (with the high rate of population growth).

3. Immigration is likely to be restricted in consumption maximizing countries to trained labor. One cannot analytically derive conditions that govern a selective immigration policy. The only rationale behind a selective immigration policy must be sought in the "free rider"-effect. Skilled migrants add to the productive capacity of a country, while the country itself does not have to pay for the training of these migrants.

4. Whether the rich country (with the low rate of population growth) allows immigration or not, the human capital stock and the physical capital stock (k_{11} and h_{11}) remain constant.

5. The brain drain from the poor country to the rich country leads, for large migration flows, to a higher physical and human capital stock in the poor country (k_{22} and h_{21}) and a lower human capital stock in the rich country (h_{11}).

To test the sensitivity of these findings for the difference in technology and training costs, a simulation has also been run for the case in which both countries have identical technologies and training costs. Qualitatively speaking the results are the same. Perhaps the most surprising result is here that $h_{21} < h_{11}$, both for the case with and without immigration.

If we now turn to the welfare analysis of a selective immigration policy we can highlight our findings by Figures 1 and 2. Figure 1 shows the (discounted) consumption levels in the case of low and differing training costs, whereas Figure 2 illustrates the case of high and identical training costs.

In the case of high and identical training costs the rich country will be better off and the poor country worse off as the immigration level increases. The reverse situation becomes apparent when the training costs are at a relatively low level and differ. If we look at the world welfare level, i.e. the sum of total discounted consumption levels of the two countries (ΣW), we can see that for large immigration flows, the world can obtain a higher welfare level. The discounted world welfare level follows a U-shaped pattern. The explanation for these opposite welfare consequences are to be found in three effects, viz. a population growth effect, a free-rider effect and a capital substitution effect. We will now deal with these effects in more detail.

1. Population growth effect. In the situations in which training costs differ and are at a low level (see Table 1 and Figure 1) an immigration policy of skilled labor by the rich country has a negative effect on the long run consumption per capita. The explanation for this state of affairs is quite simple and is in fact one of the

Figure 1:

Welfare path for various immigration levels in the case of low and differing training costs

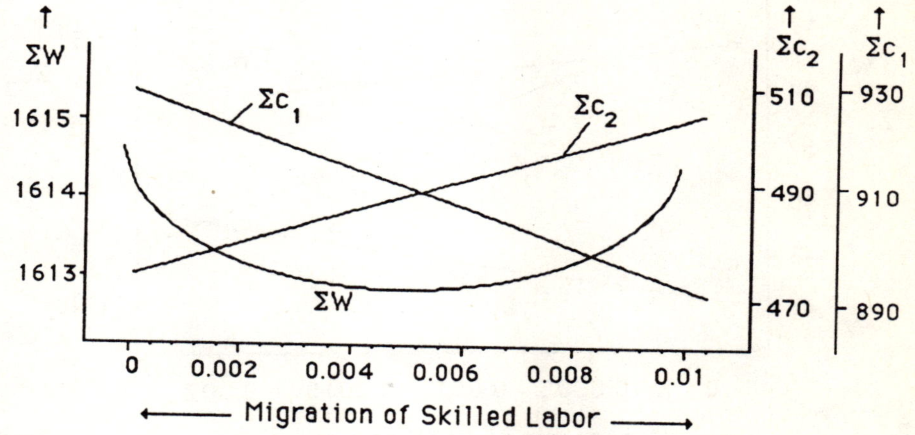

Figure 2:

Welfare path for various immigration levels in the case of high and identical training costs

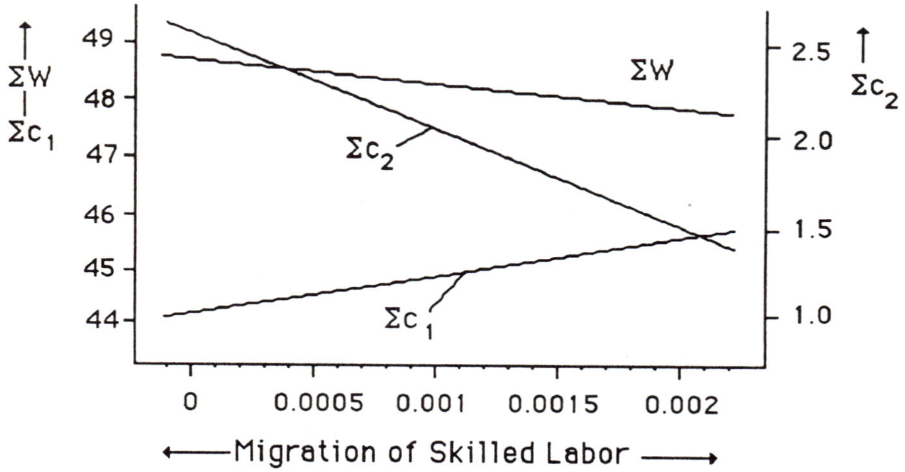

idiosyncracies of the neoclassical model. An optimal population policy within the context of the neoclassical growth model would consist of choosing the population growth rate as small as possible. As shown by van Imhoff and Ritzen (1988) there could be an effective lower bound to the extent to which the population growth rate can be profitably reduced. When the mean age of the *population* exceeds that of the *labor fource*, one can be no longer certain that a reduction of the population growth rate increases per capita consumption along optimal growth paths. The population growth effect contains elements of potential Pareto-improvements, since it was shown in van Dalen and Ritzen (1988) that any decrease in the population gap between the rich and the poor country is Pareto-efficient.

2. Free rider effect. In the situations in which educational costs are high and identical, a selective immigration policy certainly pays off for the rich country. The explanation is again straightforward. Table 2 brings the relevant aspects to the foreground. High and identical training costs in the poor country in the presence of different technologies lead to the optimal situation where the human capital accumulation per capita of the rich country is 25 times that of the poor country. This is a reflection of the assumption in the model that the marginal productivity of skilled labor is higher in developed regions than in underdeveloped regions. A migration flow of skilled labor from the poor country to the rich country leads to a considerable saving in the training efforts for the rich country. The free rider effect does not give rise to potential Pareto-improvements. On the contrary, it is Pareto-inferior as Figure 2 shows.

3. Capital substitution effect. Labor mobility is a substitute for capital mobility. An *optimal* capital transfer program coexisting with a *given* migration flow in the opposite direction will lead to smaller capital transfers than would have been the case if labor was assumed immobile. Immigration presumably is here Pareto- inferior.

The three effects, if taken together, can lead to situations in which immigration in rich countries of skilled labor from developing countries is a potential Pareto- improving policy.

5. Conclusions

The divergence in demographic development between Europe and many other parts of the world is likely to lead to selective immigration of well-trained labor from developing countries into Western Europe. The decline in the birth rate in the past decades in Western Europe can generate shortages of well-trained young workers in the labor market. Public policy might choose to counter this by selective immigration, although an expansion of (re)training efforts definitely is a viable alternative.

The present study has brought into the foreground a few of the implications of an immigration policy. The optimal two-country growth model by van Dalen and Ritzen (1988) served as a benchmark. The main conclusion implied by this model was that the rich country, with the low rate of population growth will constantly increase its capital holdings in the poor country, i.e. the country with the high rate of populatioin growth. Both will gain by engaging in international capital market transactions.

Introduction of optimal human capital formation and the possibility of labor mobility points out that the determination of welfare gains and losses of migration is an ambiguous affair. The analysis shows that the ambiguity results from three effects. These are the effects of changes in the effective population growth rate, a free rider effect in the country of immigration and a capital substitution effect. The latter implies that physical capital investment by rich countries in poor countries declines with immigration. The net result of these effects in terms of welfare of each of the countries and total world welfare depends heavily on the technologies in use and the cost of training.

By comparing welfare levels of the world with and without migration, it turns out that a constant migration flow from the country with the high population growth rate to the country with the low population growth rate is an inferior policy in the strict Paretian sense. i.e. one country is always worse off compared to the regime of capital mobility. When optimal training efforts are a small share of gross national product discounted world welfare follows a U-shaped pattern for various immigration flows. Thus, for large migration flows there exists a *potential* Pareto improvement compared to the case of mobile capital but immobile labor.

When training efforts require a large share of the gross national product discounted world welfare is always smaller when migration is allowed. This is a consequence of the fact that the smaller part of the world is enjoying more consumption than it did in the restricted labor mobility case, while the larger part of the world is enjoying less.

References

Bhagwati, J.N. (ed.)(1976), **The Brain Drain and Taxation, Theory and Empirical Analysis**, Vol. II, Amsterdam, North-Holland.

——— (1978), **International Migration of the Highly Skilled: Economics, Ethics and Tax Arrangements**, mimeo., M.I.T., Cambridge, Mass.

Bhagwati, J.N. and M. Partington (eds.) (1976), **Taxing the Brain Drain, A Proposal**, Vol. I, Amsterdam, North-Holland.

Bhagwati, J.N. and C.A. Rodriguez (1976), Welfare-Theoretical Analyses of the Brain Drain, in: J.N. Bhagwati (ed.), The Brain Drain and Taxation, Theory and Empirical Analysis, Vol. II, 85-111.

Brecher, R.A. and E.U. Choudhri (1987), International Migration versus Foreign Investment in the Presence of Unemployment, in: **Journal of International Economics**, 23, 329-342.

Central Bureau of Statistics (1988), **CBS Bulletin No. 8**, The Hague.

Central Planning Bureau (1983), **Vooruitberekening van het trendmatige arbeidsaanbod tussen 1980 en 2010** (trans.: Calculation of the structural growth in labour supply between 1980 and 2010), Monografie 24, The Hague.

van Dalen, H.P. and J.M.M. Ritzen (1988), **Economic Growth in a World of Diverging Populations**, Discussion Paper No. 8809/P, Institute for Economic Research, Erasmus University Rotterdam.

Foot, D.K. (1986), **Population Aging and Immigration Policy in Canada: Implications and Presciptions**, Working Paper no. 8606, Institute for Policy Analysis, University of Toronto.

Foreman-Peck, J. (1983), **A History of the World Economy, International Economic Relations since 1850**, Brighton, Harvester Press.

Greenwood, M.J. (1985), Human Migration: Theory, Models and Empirical Studies, in: **Journal of Regional Science**, 25, 521-544.

Heijke, J.A.M. (1987), The Labour Market Position of Migrants in Selected European Receiving Countries, in: **The Future of Migration**, Paris, OECD.

van Imhoff, E. (1989), **Optimal Economic Growth and Investment in Education under** Conditions of Non-Stable Population, in: Journal of Human Resources, forthcoming.

van Imhoff, E. and J.M.M. Ritzen (1988), Optimal Economic Growth and Non-stable Population, in: **De Economist**, 136, 339-357.

Prescott, E.C. and J.H. Boyd (1987), Dynamic Coalitions: Engines of Growth, in: **American Economic Review, Papers and Proceedings**, 77, 63-77.

Ritzen, J.M.M. (1977), **Education, Economic Growth and Income Distribution**, Amsterdam, North-Holland.

——— (ed.)(1985), **Menselijk kapitaal en conjunctuur** (trans.: Human Capital and Business Cycles), Institute for Fiscal and Public Sector Economics, Erasmus University Rotterdam.

Rodriguez, C.A. (1975), On the Welfare Aspects of International Migration, in: **Journal of Political Economy**, 83, 1065-1072.

——— (1976), Brain Drain and Economic Growth: A Dynamic Model, in: J.N. Bhagwati (ed.) The Brain Drain and Taxation, Theory and Empirical Analysis, Vol. II, 171-195.

Schütze, H.G. and D. Instance (eds.) (1988), **Recurrent Education Revisited**, Stockholm, Almqvist and Wicksell.

Sjaastad, L.A. (1960), The Relationship between Migration and Income in the United States, in: **Papers and Proceedings of the Regional Science Association**, 6, 37-64.

Tu, P.N.V. (1988), **Migration: Gains or Losses?**, mimeo., University of Calgary.

Wilkinson, M. (1970), European Migration to the United States: An Econometric Analysis of Aggregate Labor Supply and Demand, in: **Review of Economics and Statistics**, 52, 272-279.

List of Contributors

Siegfried Berninghaus, *University of Mannheim*, Mannheim, Germany

Hendrik P. van Dalen, *University of Rotterdam*, Rotterdam, The Netherlands

Jiang Hong Li, *Louisiana State University*, Baton Rouge, USA

Lucie Merkle, *University of Munich*, Munich, Germany

Jozef M. M. Ritzen, *University of Rotterdam*, Rotterdam, and *Minister of Education*, The Netherlands

Christoph M. Schmidt, *University of Munich*, Munich, Germany

Gerhard Schmitt-Rink, *University of Bochum*, Bochum, Germany

Renate Schubert, *University of Darmstadt*, Darmstadt, Germany

Hans-Günther Seifert-Vogt, *University of Konstanz*, Konstanz, Germany

Joachim Singelmann, *Louisiana State University*, Baton Rouge, USA

Thomas Straubhaar, *University of Basel*, Basel, Switzerland

Klaus F. Zimmermann, *University of Munich*, Munich, Germany and CEPR, London, United Kingdom

Printing: Druckhaus Beltz, Hemsbach
Binding: Buchbinderei Kränkl, Heppenheim